GOVERNANCE OF THE JURIST
(Velayat-e Faqeeh)

ISLAMIC GOVERNMENT

IMĀM KHOMEINI

Publisher:
The Institute for Compilation and Publication of
Imam Khomeini's Works
(International Affairs Division)

Translator and Annotator: Hamid Algar

Proofread and typeset by: Mansoor L. Limba

Address: P.O. Box 19575 / 614, Tehran,

Islamic Republic of Iran

1

Table of Contents

2

FOREWORD

In the name of God, the Compassionate, the Merciful

All praise be to God; there is neither might nor strength but from God, the Exalted, the Sublime. May peace and blessings be upon the Messenger of God, Muhammad, the Seal of the Prophets, and his purified progeny.

The present book, *Governance of the Jurist*, including relevant footnotes and explanations, is the compendium of thirteen speeches of His Eminence Imām Khomeini delivered during his stay in Najaf from January 21 to February 8, 1970. Now, this book is presented to the knowledgeable researchers and those ardent of the works of Imām Khomeini. These speeches had been reproduced and disseminated then in various forms as lessons and instruction materials. Later, in autumn of 1970 the texts of the speeches were edited and prepared for printing. Following the approval of Imām Khomeini, it was printed in Beirut (Lebanon) by Imām Khomeini's friends, then secretly sent to Iran, while copies of which were simultaneously sent to the revolutionary Muslims in Europe, United States, Pakistan, and Afghanistan. In 1977, before the victory of the Islamic Revolution, the book was published in Iran entitled, *A Letter from Imām Mūsāwi Kāshif al-Ghitā* and *Jihād-i Akbar* as its supplement. Like the other works of Imām Khomeini, the book *Governance of the Jurist* had been considered on top of the list of prohibited books for publication during the Shāh's regime. So many people were imprisoned and tortured on the charge of publishing, possessing, or reading the book. However, despite all pressures exerted by the SAVAK (the Shāh's notorious secret police) and restraints imposed by the Shāh's regime, the notion to support the establishment of an Islamic government whose legislative principles are expounded here by Imām Khomeini, gained a widespread adherence among the revolutionary Muslim forces at the religious seminaries, universities and other notable centers; and with the 15th of Khurdād uprising and Imām Khomeini's movement, the idea of establishing an Islamic government based on *governance of the jurist* was crystallized as a fundamental idea. The Islamic jurists (*fuqahā*) have generally been involved in the issue of *governance of the jurist* in different subject matters in *fiqh*, some briefly and some in details. However, no comprehensive and orderly discourse is found in the *fiqh* books of predecessors; the reason being the unfavorable political and social conditions prevailing over Islamic countries in the past and the dominance of tyrannical ruling cliques that had made it impossible to touch upon such discussions. But regardless of the difference among *fuqahā* on the extent of authorities and the case applicability of *governance of the jurist* during the period of Occultation,[*] there is unanimity among them in general as to the affirmation of a certain kind of guardianship authority for the fully competent *faqīh*. Opinions of *fuqahā* on the kind of guardianship and the extent of authorities of the Islamic jurists during the period of Occultation have been recently compiled and published in some books.

According to available sources, the late Āyatullāh Mullā Ahmad Narāqi[**] (one of the Qājār dynasty contemporary scholars) has dealt with this subject matter in his book *'Awā'id al-Ayyām* more detailed than the others. He first tried to seek evidence

---

from numerous narrations proving that the *faqīh* is entrusted with guardianship rights during the Occultation period in the following areas:

1. In all instances, where the Prophet and the infallible Imāms ('a) had been authorized and assigned as guardians except in cases, where this had been excluded due to religiously legal requirement.

2. In all instances related to religious and living duties of people that must be carried out.

By relying on Qur'anic verses, Prophetic traditions, and jurisprudential arguments, he continues the discourse by giving ten examples of applicable cases within the sphere of governance of the jurist such as *iftā*; administering punishment; protecting the properties of the orphans, insane, and the absent individuals; and taking possession of properties of the infallible Imāms.

Although it can be understood from the late Narāqi's discussions that he has included governance within the same sphere, he has not openly stressed on it.

After the late Narāqi, Imām Khomeini was the only *faqīh* to deal tacitly with the *governance of the jurist* for the first time and proved the point. As indicated earlier, Imām Khomeini had once discussed the question of *governance of the jurist* in Najaf in thirteen instructional sessions of which the present book is the transcription and edited form of the same course instructions. He further discussed *governance of the jurist* in the second volume of his five-volume book entitled, *Kitāb al-Bay'* in the same profound style.

In the present book, *Governance of the Jurist*, Imām Khomeini has laid great emphasis on guardianship (*wilāyat*) as a principle, serving as the base and foundation for all duties. He especially examines guardianship from governmental and political points of view. Here, in addition to expounding the political and social factors causing the neglect of the most important Islamic issue, he has methodologically examined the question, and based on the same sturdy approach exercised in *fiqh*, proceeded with introductory practicable programs for realization of *governance of the jurist* in the government.

He begins by disclosing the plots and conspiracies made by the enemies to annihilate Islam. Then he continues logically to discuss insinuated misgivings, such as "Islam is not a competent religion to govern the society at the age of industrial civilization" or "legal provisions of Islam are inadequate to resolve the social problems, and to provide us with appropriate answers".

In this regard Imām Khomeini points out that the misgivings suggested by the enemies to pave the way for the faulty notion of separation of religion from politics, have unfortunately been so much effective; even in the seminaries, one dares not to speak freely about the Islamic government. He further indicated the domestic shortcomings and infatuations for the new civilization, all of which are the souvenir of the devilish propaganda of imperialism. He warned the seminaries, the young clergy students, and the Muslim thinkers to endeavor enormously to carry out their political and social duties and be careful not to be deceived. Islam is not opposed to technological and industrial progress; but social problems require ethical and religious solution, and Islam is that all-embracing religion that can solve all problems, provided the thinkers and scholars of the Islamic world would face the challenge.

By expounding the indisputable historical fact that the Most Noble Messenger (s) had appointed a successor, Imām Khomeini posed the question of "whether the successor had been designed just to expound the religious precepts." Of course not! Expounding religious precepts does not require to be done by the Prophet's successor. Therefore the appointment had been for rulership, and for enforcement of laws and

4

regulations. It is most important now to believe in the necessity to establish an Islamic government; thus, we can determine the position and role of the successor.

In this book Imām Khomeini has given some instances proving the necessity for establishing an Islamic government, as follows:

1. Action taken by the Holy Prophet (s) to establish a government;
2. The fact that divine precepts are to be enforced perpetually; they are enacted not only for the time of the Holy Prophet (s); they are meant for all time.
3. The nature and characteristic of Islamic laws and regulations like fiscal, national defense, and legal and penal precepts are such that they are not executable without a government.

After giving quite well-reasoned explanation on the necessity of Islamic government, Imām Khomeini refers to the historical background of deviation from this principle during the Umayyad period and its continuation during the Abbasids who had adopted un-Islamic rule, imitating the Iranian monarchical, Roman imperial and the Egyptian pharaonic systems. And the same way continued afterwards. He stresses on the logical demand for alteration of such systems, and that it is therefore necessary to stir up a political revolution. Accordingly, it is necessary to revolt against tyrannical governments to pave the way for the establishment of Islamic government and the enforcement of Islamic precepts, unification of Islamic *ummah* that have now fallen into the trap of disunity caused by various domestic elements as well as foreigners, and finally, to save the oppressed and the deprived people as a religious duty of all Muslims, especially the scholars. Imām Khomeini further continues emphasizing on the necessity of establishing an Islamic government, by relating the subject to a narration quoted by Fadl ibn Shādān on the philosophy of ordaining governments as provided for in the narration and traditions.

An important part of the book deals with the difference between an Islamic government and other types of governments, pointing out that the Islamic government is a special kind of constitutional government that is anchored on the Islamic laws. Imām Khomeini believes, therefore, that Islamic legislative power or law-making assemblies are bound to devise all governmental plans and programs within the framework of Islamic precepts; not according to regular procedures followed by other states.

Imām Khomeini further deals with the prerequisite qualities of the ruler, as derived directly from the nature of Islamic government. In addition to the regular requirement such as intelligence and prudence, there are two principal prerequisites for the ruler: his knowledge about the law and his justness.

Governance of the *faqīh* during the Occultation is the next to be dealt with. Following the previous discussion, Imām Khomeini says, "Now we live at the Occultation period. On the one hand, Islamic precepts are to be enforced, (and no one is designated by God Almighty to fulfill this task), and on the other hand, what should we do then?" He examines this subject matter and comes to the conclusion that "God Almighty has given the quality which is required for rulership to a great number of religious scholars from the very outset of Islam to the advent of the Imām of the Age ('a). This quality is the knowledge about law and justice. A great number of our contemporary scholars (*fuqahā*) possess this quality and they should join hands. They will be able to establish a just government in the world." He then points out that governance of the jurist is an extrinsic and rational issue, and the fully competent *faqīh* is entrusted with all the authorities; that the Prophet and the infallible Imāms ('a) were entitled too, for governance; and that this guardianship cannot be realized except through entitlement and that it implies in itself no dignity and status, but only a means of carrying out one's duty and enforcing religious precepts.

The exalted aims of government, and characteristics required for the ruler are then referred to. Relying on traditions, Imām Khomeini deduces that *governance of the jurist* implies entitlement to government as well as argumentation that constitutes the greater part of the book. The concluding part of the book deals with the necessity for a long-range planning to achieve this divine objective. Here, Imām Khomeini points out the importance of propagation and instructions, while saying, "Meetings must be directed to serve these two important tasks. Struggles must be stirred as 'Āshūrā to create waves of crowds insisting on the establishment of Islamic government, and prepared for a long-term struggle while not bearing in mind an immediate achievement".

The necessity for proper attention to instructions and propagations, moral and cultural reformation of seminaries, annihilation of the moral and cultural effects of imperialism, correction of the pseudo-saints, purging the seminaries of the court 'ulamā, and finally, taking effective measures to overthrow the oppressive and tyrannical governments, are among the concluding discussions of the book.

Esteemed readers' attentions are drawn to the fact that after his divine uprising, which, thanks to the divine grace, consciousness and unity of the Muslim people, gained victory over monarchical system in Iran on Bahman 22, 1358 Sh./February 11, 1979, Imām Khomeini undertook the leadership of the Islamic Revolution and the guardianship function of the nation. It should, therefore, be taken into consideration that comprehending precisely Imām Khomeini's viewpoints on governance of the jurist, which is explained in this book, can only be realized when full consideration is given to his personal manners and conducts in the course of his rule and his ideas about the extent of authorities and the station of guardianship as expressed through his speeches, messages and letters.[*]

"O God, foreshorten the arms of the oppressors that are stretched out against the lands of the Muslims and root out all traitors to Islam and the Islamic countries. Awaken the heads of the Muslims states from their deep sleep so that they may exert themselves on behalf of their people's interests and renounce divisiveness and the quest for personal gain. Grant that the younger generation studying in the religious colleges and the universities may struggle to reach the sacred aims of Islam and strive together, with ranks united, first, to deliver the Islamic countries from the clutches of imperialism and its vile agents, and then to defend them. Grant that the *fuqahā* and the scholars may strive to guide and enlighten the minds of the people, to convey the sacred aims of Islam to all Muslims, particularly the younger generation, and to struggle for the establishment of an Islamic government. From You is success, and there is neither recourse nor strength except in God, the Exalted, the Sublime."[*]

The Institute for Compilation and Publication
of Imām Khomeini's Works

---

[*] A collection of the viewpoints and stances on this argumentation is being compiled by this Institute.
[*] The written supplication at the end of the present volume.

INTRODUCTI<

THE SUBJECT OF THE GOVERNANCE OF THE JURIST *(vilāyat-i faqīh[160])* provides us with the opportunity to discuss certain related matters and questions. The governance of the *faqīh* is a subject that in itself elicits immediate assent and has little need of demonstration, for anyone who has some general awareness of the beliefs and ordinances of Islam will unhesitatingly give his assent to the principle of the governance of the *faqīh* as soon as he encounters it; he will recognize it as necessary and self-evident. If little attention is paid to this principle today, so that it has come to require demonstration, it is because of the social circumstances prevailing among the Muslims in general, and the teaching institution in particular. These circumstances, in turn, have certain historical roots to which I will now briefly refer.

From the very beginning, the historical movement of Islam has had to contend with the Jews, for it was they who first established anti-Islamic propaganda and engaged in various stratagems, and as you can see, this activity continues down to the present. Later they were joined by other groups, who were in certain respects, more satanic than they. These new groups began their imperialist penetration of the Muslim countries about three hundred years ago,[1a] and they regarded it as necessary to work for the extirpation of Islam in order to attain their ultimate goals. It was not their aim to alienate the people from Islam in order to promote Christianity among them, for the imperialists really have no religious belief, Christian or Islamic. Rather, throughout this long historical period, and going back to the Crusades,[1b] they felt that the major obstacle in the path of their materialistic ambitions and the chief threat to their political power was nothing but Islam and its ordinances, and the belief of the people in Islam. They therefore plotted and campaigned against Islam by various means.

The preachers they planted in the religious teaching institution, the agents they employed in the universities, government educational institutions, and publishing houses, and the orientalists who work in the service of the imperialistic states—all these people have pooled their energies in an effort to distort the principles of Islam.

---

[160] *Faqīh*: one learned in the principles and ordinances of Islamic law, or more generally, in all aspects of the faith. For a full discussion of the term, see p. 69-70.

[1a] Since mid-16th century, i.e., more than three centuries ago when the Portuguese and thereafter the Dutch, English, French, Italian, and the Spaniards colonized uslim countries. At the beginning, newly discovered African countries and then, after finding the sea routes, Asian countries (whose link with the Europeans had been curtailed since the Ottoman conquest of Constantinople in 1453) fell under the sway of colonialism. [Pub.]

[1b] Crusades is the name of a series of war campaigns waged by the European Christians against the Muslims (11th-13th centuries) for the control of the Holy Land, particularly Jerusalem. Waged in eight stages, these campaigns commenced with the religious edict of Pope Urban II at the Council of Clermont (1096/489) and ended with the death of the French King, Saint Louis IX (1214-70) in 1270/669. Owing to the red-colored piece of cloth in the form of cross embedded on their right shoulders, the Christians became known as the Army of the Cross, or Crusaders. [Pub.]

As a result, many persons, particularly the educated, have formed misguided and incorrect notions of Islam.

Islam is the religion of militant individuals who are committed to truth and justice. It is the religion of those who desire freedom and independence. It is the school of those who struggle against imperialism. But the servants of imperialism have presented Islam in a totally different light. They have created in men's minds a false notion of Islam. The defective version of Islam, which they have presented in the religious teaching institution, is intended to deprive Islam of its vital, revolutionary aspect and to prevent Muslims from arousing themselves in order to gain their freedom, fulfill the ordinances of Islam, and create a government that will assure their happiness and allow them to live, lives worthy of human beings.

For example, the servants of imperialism declared that Islam is not a comprehensive religion providing for every aspect of human life and has no laws or ordinances pertaining to society. It has no particular form of government. Islam concerns itself only with rules of ritual purity after menstruation and parturition. It may have a few ethical principles, but it certainly has nothing to say about human life in general and the ordering of society.

This kind of evil propaganda has unfortunately had an effect. Quite apart from the masses, the educated class—university students and also many students at the religious teaching institutions—have failed to understand Islam correctly and have erroneous notions. Just as people may, in general, be unacquainted with a stranger, so too they are unacquainted with Islam. Islam lives among the people of this world as if it were a stranger.[161] If somebody were to present Islam as it truly is, he would find it difficult to make people believe him. In fact, the agents of imperialism in the religious teaching institutions would raise a hue and cry against him.

In order to demonstrate to some extent, the difference between Islam and what is presented as Islam, I would like to draw your attention to the difference between the Holy Qur'an and the books of *hadīth*,[162] on the one hand, and the practical treatises of jurisprudence, on the other. The Holy Qur'an and the books of *hadīth*, which represent the sources for the commands and ordinances of Islam, are completely different from the treatises written by the *mujtahīds*[163] of the present age both in breadth of scope and in the effects they are capable of exerting on the life of society. The ratio of Qur'anic verses concerned with the affairs of society to those concerned with ritual worship is greater than a hundred to one. Of the approximately fifty sections[4a] of the corpus of *hadīth* containing all the ordinances of Islam, not more than three or four sections relate to matters of ritual worship and the duties of man toward his Creator and Sustainer. A few more are concerned with questions of ethics, and all the rest are concerned with social, economic, legal, and political questions—in short, the gestation of society.

---

[161] This is an allusion to the celebrated saying of the Prophet: "Islam will again become a stranger among men, as it was in the beginning, but blessed is the state of the stranger."

[162] *Hadīth*: a tradition setting forth a saying or deed of the Prophet, or in Shī'i usage, of one of the Twelve Imāms.

[163] *Mujtahīd*: an authority on divine law who practices *ijtihād*, that is, "the search for a correct opinion...in the deducing of the specific provisions of the law from its principles and ordinances" (Muhammad Sanglaji, *Qazā dar Islam* [Tehran, 1338 Sh./1959], p.14).

[4a] The term *kitāb* ("book") in the parlance of the Islamic jurists and traditionists means "section" in which Prophetic narrations (*ahādīth*) pertaining to a single topic are collected or particular laws of a topic, are discussed, such as *Kitāb at-Tawhīd*, *Kitāb al-Īmān wa 'l-Fikr*, *Kitāb as-Salāh*, and others. For instance, in the *hadīth* literature, *Dūreh-ye Kāfi* consists of 35 books, and in jurisprudence, *Sharā'i 'ul-Islām* comprises 50 books. [Pub.]

You who represent the younger generation and who, God willing, will be of service to Islam in the future must strive diligently all your lives to pursue the aims I will now set forth and to impart the laws and ordinances of Islam. In whatever way you deem most beneficial, in writing or in speech, instruct the people about the problems Islam has had to contend with since its inception and about the enemies and afflictions that now threaten it. Do not allow the true nature of Islam to remain hidden, or people will imagine that Islam is like Christianity (nominal, not true Christianity), a collection of injunctions pertaining to man's relation to God, and the mosques will be equated with the church.

At a time when the West was a realm of darkness and obscurity—with its inhabitants living in a state of barbarism, and America still peopled by half-savaged redskins—and the two vast empires of Iran and Byzantium were under the rule of tyranny, class privilege, and discrimination, and the powerful dominated all without any trace of law or popular government, God, Exalted and Almighty, by means of the Most Noble Messenger (s), sent laws that astound people with their magnitude. He instituted laws and practices for all human affairs and laid injunctions for man extending from even before the embryo is formed until after he is placed in the tomb. In just the same way that there are laws setting forth the duties of worship for man, so too there are laws, practices, and norms for the affairs of society and government. Islamic law is a progressive, evolving, and comprehensive system. All the voluminous books that have been compiled from the earliest times on different areas of law, such as judicial procedure, social transactions, penal law,[4b] retribution,[4c] international relations, regulations pertaining to peace and war, private and public law—taken together, these contain a mere sample of the laws and injunctions of Islam. There is not a single topic in human life for which Islam has not provided instructions and established a norm.

In order to make the Muslims, especially the intellectuals, and the younger generation, deviate from the path of Islam, foreign agents have constantly insinuated that Islam has nothing to offer, that Islam consists of a few ordinances concerning menstruation and parturition, and that this is the proper field of study for the *ākhūnds*.[164]

There is something of truth here, for it is fitting that those *ākhūnds* who have no intention of expounding the theories, injunctions and worldview of Islam and who spend most of their time on precisely such matters, forgetting all the other topics of Islamic law, be attacked and accused in this manner. They too are at fault; foreigners are not the only ones to be blamed. For several centuries, as might be expected, the foreigners laid certain plans to realize their political and economic ambitions, and the neglect that has overtaken the religious teaching institution has made it possible for them to succeed. There have been individuals among us, the *'ulamā*,[165] who have unwittingly contributed to the fulfillment of those aims, with the result that you now see.

[4b] *Hadd* (literally means limit, boundary or limit) in the Islamic law is generally applied for penal law for punishments prescribed for particular crimes. The extent of these punishments is determined by law. [Pub.]

[4c] *Qisās* (literally means retribution or retaliation) in the Islamic jurisprudence is to be executed against a criminal, according to the legal decree, who committed such crime as murder, amputation of a body limb, or laceration and beating in case the victim or his guardians are seeking retribution in lieu of receiving fine or blood money. [Pub.]

[164] *Ākhūnd*: a word of uncertain etymology that originally denoted a scholar of unusual attainment, but was later applied to lesser-ranking scholars, and then acquired a pejorative connotation, particularly in secularist usage.

[165] *'Ulamā*: the scholars of Islam.

It is sometimes insinuated that the injunctions of Islam are defective, and said that the laws of judicial procedure, for example, are not all that they should be. In keeping with this insinuation and propaganda, agents of Britain were instructed by their masters to take advantage of the idea of constitutionalism in order to deceive the people and conceal the true nature of their political crimes (the pertinent proofs and documents are now available). At the beginning of the constitutional movement, when people wanted to write laws and draw up a constitution, a copy of the Belgian legal code was borrowed from the Belgian embassy and a handful of individuals (whose names I do not wish to mention here) used it as the basis for the constitution they then wrote, supplementing its deficiencies with borrowings from the French and British legal codes.[166] True, they added some of the ordinances of Islam in order to deceive the people, but the basis of the laws that were now thrust upon the people was alien and borrowed.

What connections do all the various articles of the Constitution as well as the body of Supplementary Law[167] concerning the monarchy, the succession, and so forth, have with Islam? They are all opposed to Islam; they violate the system of government and the laws of Islam.

Islam proclaims monarchy and hereditary succession wrong and invalid. When Islam first appeared in Iran, the Byzantine Empire, Egypt, and the Yemen, the entire institution of monarchy was abolished. In the blessed letters that the Most Noble Messenger (s) wrote to the Byzantine Emperor Heraclius and the Shāhanshāh of Iran,[168] he called upon them to abandon the monarchical and imperial form of

---

[166] The draft of the first constitution was written by a commission from among the members of the Parliament and was approved with 51 articles. Kasravi, in this connection, writes: "It seems that Mashīr ad-Dawlah and Mu'tamīn al-Mulk and sons of Sadr A'zam wrote it, or to be more appropriate, we say they translated [it]." Thereafter, a committee was formed so that a text called "Supplement" be appended in the constitution. By the way, this text was prepared in 107 articles. According to the narration of Mustafā Rahīmi, "With the use of the Belgian constitution and to some extent, the French constitution, and taking into account the laws of the Balkan states (in view of the newness of the supplementary laws under consideration), the committee embarked on the compilation of the Supplementary Constitutional Laws and on the omission of flaws of the former laws." Concerning this influence of Belgian constitutional law on the six-man committee that drafted the Supplementary Constitutional Laws of 1907, see A.K.S. Lambton, "Dustur, iv: Iran," *Encyclopedia of Islam* new ed., II, 653-654; Kasravi Tabrizi, *Tārīkh-i Mashrūteh-yi Īrān* (Constitutional History of Iran), pp. 170, 224; Mustafā Rahīmi, *Qānūn-i Asāsi-yi Īrān va Usūl-i Demokrāsi* (The Constitution of Iran and Democratic Principles) (Tehran, 1347 Sh./1968), p. 94; *Qānūn-i Asāsi va Mutammim Ān* (The Constituion and Its Supplement) (Tehran: National Consultative Assembly Press). [Pub.]

[167] Articles 35 through 57 of the Supplementary Constitutional Laws approved on October 7, 1906 relate to "the rights of the throne." See E.G. Browne, *The Persian Revolution of 1905-1909* (Cambridge, 1911), pp. 337-379.

[168] In the seventh year of the Islamic era, Prophet Muhammad wrote not only to Heraclius and the ruler of Iran (probably Parvīz), but also to the rulers of Egypt and Abyssinia, inviting them all to embrace Islam and abandon unjust rule. Following is the text of the Most Noble Messenger's letter to Khosroe Parviz:

"In the name of Allah, the Beneficent, the Merciful. From Muhammad, the Messenger of Allah, to the great Kisra of Iran. Peace be upon him, who seeks truth and expresses belief in Allah and in His Prophet and testifies that there is no god but Allah and that He has no partner, and who believes that Muhammad is His servant and Prophet. Under the Command of Allah, I invite you to Him. He has sent me for the guidance of all people so that I may warn them all of His wrath and may present the unbelievers with an ultimatum. Embrace Islam so that you may remain safe. And if you refuse to accept Islam, you will be responsible for the sins of the Magi."

Text of his letter to Heraclius is as follows:

"In the name of Allah, the Beneficent, the Merciful. "(This is a letter) from Muhammad ibn 'Abdullāh to the great Hercules of Rome. Peace be upon the followers of guidance. I invite you to the religion of Islam. Embrace Islam so that you may be safe. Allah will give you two rewards (reward for

government, to cease compelling the servants of God to worship them with absolute obedience, and to permit men to worship God, Who has no partner and is the True Monarch. Monarchy and hereditary succession represent the same sinister, evil system of government that prompted the Doyen of the Martyrs[169] ('a) to rise up in revolt and seek martyrdom in an effort to prevent its establishment. He revolted in repudiation of the hereditary succession of Yazīd,[170] to refuse it his recognition.

Islam, then, does not recognize monarchy and hereditary succession; they have no place in Islam. If that is what is meant by the so-called deficiency of Islam, then Islam is indeed deficient. Islam has laid down no laws for the practice of usury, for banking on the basis of usury, for the consumption of alcohol, or for the cultivation of sexual vice, having radically prohibited all of these. The ruling cliques, therefore, who are the puppets of imperialism and wish to promote these vices in the Islamic world, will naturally regard Islam as defective. They must import the appropriate laws from Britain, France, Belgium, and most recently, America. The fact that Islam makes no provision for the orderly pursuit of these illicit activities, far from being a deficiency, is a sign of perfection and a source of pride.

The conspiracy worked out by the imperialist government of Britain at the beginning of the constitutional movement had two purposes. The first, which was already known at that time, was to eliminate the influence of Tsarist Russia in Iran, and the second was to take the laws of Islam out of force and operation by introducing Western laws.[171]

The imposition of foreign laws on our Islamic society has been the source of numerous problems and difficulties. Knowledgeable people working in our judicial system have many complaints concerning the existing laws and their mode of operation. If a person becomes caught up in the judicial system of Iran or that of analogous countries, he may have to spend a whole lifetime trying to prove his case. In my youth I once encountered a learned lawyer who said, "I can spend my whole life following a litigation back and forth through the judicial machinery, and then

---

your own faith as well as reward for the faith of those who are your subordinates). In case, however, you turn away your face from Islam you will be responsible for the sins of the Arisiyans as well. "O people of the Scriptures! We invite you to a common basis i.e., we should not worship anyone except Allah. We should not treat anyone to be His partner. Some of us too should not accept others as their gods. And (O Muhammad! as and when) they become recalcitrant against the true religion say: "Be witness to the fact that we are Muslims [Q 3:64]." "

See *Makātib ar*-Rasūl, vol. 1, pp. 90 and 105; Ja'far Subhāni, *The* Message (Karachi: Islamic Seminary Publications, 1984), chap. 42, pp. 540-566, Muhammad Hamidullah, *Le Prophète de l'Islam* (Paris, 1959), I, 196-197, 212, 230, 241. [Pub.]

[169] The Doyen of the Martyrs: Imām Husayn, grandson of the Prophet. Concerning his biography, see Mīr Ahmad 'Ali, *Husain the Saviour of Islam* (Qum: Ansariyan Publications, 1987); 'Abdullāh Yūsuf 'Ali, *Imām Husain and His Martyrdom* [Pub.]

[170] In 60/680, Imām Husayn refused to swear allegiance to Yazīd, son of Mu'āwiyah and second caliph of the Umayyad dynasty, since Yazīd did not possess legitimate authority and had succeeded to the caliphate by hereditary succession. The ensuing death of the Imām in battle at Karbala has always been commemorated by Shī'ah Muslims as the supreme example of martyrdom in the face of tyranny. It served as an important point of both ideological and emotive reference throughout the Islamic Revolution in Iran. See Shaykh Muhammad Mahdi Shams ad-Dīn, *The Revolution of Al-Husayn*, Ibrāhīm Āyāti, *A Probe into the History of Āshūrā* (Karachi: Islamic Seminary Publications, 1984); Zākir, *Tears and Tributes* (Qum: Ansariyan Publications); Yāsīn T. al-Jibouri, *Kerbala and Beyond* (Qum: Ansariyan Publications); Sayyid Wāhid Akhtar, "Karbala: An Enduring Paradigm of Islamic Revivalism," *Al-Tawhīd Journal* [Pub.]

[171] No detailed study has yet been made of the British role in the early part of the constitutional movement. Some of the relevant documents, however, are to be found in *General Report on Persia for the Year 1906* (file F.O. 416/30, Public Records Office, London).

bequeath it to my son for him to do the same thing!" That is the situation that now prevails, except, of course, when one of the parties has influence, in which case the matter is examined and settled swiftly, albeit unjustly.

Our present judicial laws have brought our people nothing but trouble, causing them to neglect their daily task and providing the occasion for all kinds of misuse. Very few people are able to obtain their legitimate rights. In the adjudication of cases, it is necessary not only that everyone should obtain his rights, but also that correct procedure be followed. People's time must be considered, as well as the way of life and profession of both parties, so that matters are resolved as swiftly and simply as possible.

A case that a *sharī'ah*[172] judge in earlier times settled in one or two days cannot be settled now in twenty years. The needy, young, and old alike, must spend the entire day at the Ministry of Justice, from morning to evening, wasting their time in corridors or standing in front of some official's desk, and in the end they will still not know what has transpired. Anyone who is more cunning, and more willing and able to give bribes, has his case settled expeditiously, but at the cost of justice. Otherwise, they must wait in frustration and perplexity until their entire lives are gone.

The agents of imperialism sometimes write in their books and their newspapers that the legal provisions of Islam are too harsh. One person was even so impudent as to write that the laws of Islam are harsh because they have originated with the Arabs, so that the "harshness" of the Arabs is reflected in the harshness of Islamic law!

I am amazed at the way these people think. They kill people for possessing ten grams of heroin and say, "That is the law" (I have been informed that ten people were put to death some time ago, and another person more recently, for possession of ten grams of heroin).[173] Inhuman laws like this are concocted in the name of a campaign against corruption, and they are not to be regarded as harsh. (I am not saying it is permissible to sell heroin, but this is not the appropriate punishment. The sale of heroin must indeed be prohibited but the punishment must be in proportion to the crime.)[14a] When Islam, however, stipulates that the drinker of alcohol should receive eighty lashes, they consider it "too harsh." They can *execute* someone for possessing ten grams of heroin and the question of harshness does not even arise!

Many forms of corruption that have appeared in society derive from alcohol. The collisions that take place on our roads, and the murders and suicides are very often caused by the consumption of alcohol. Indeed, even the use of heroin is said to derive from addiction to alcohol. But still, some say, it is quiet unobjectionable for someone to drink alcohol (after all, they do it in the West); so let alcohol be bought and sold freely.

But when Islam wishes to prevent the consumption of alcohol—one of the major evils—stipulating that the drinker should receive eighty lashes, or sexual vice, decreeing that the fornicator be given one hundred lashes (and the married man or

---

[172] *Sharī'ah*: the all-embracing law of Islam derived from the Qur'an, the normative practice and authoritative pronouncements of the Prophet, and a number of secondary sources.

[173] A law promulgated in July 1969 provided the death penalty for anyone in possession of more than two kilograms of opium or ten grams of heroin, morphine, or cocaine. The first ten executions were carried out in December 1969 and by 1974, 236 people had been executed on charges under this law. See Ulrich Gehrke, *Iran: Natur, Bevolkerung, Geschichte, Kultur, Staat, Wirschaft* (Tubingen and Basel, 1976), p. 281. It is also probable that the law was also used to provide a cover for the execution of political prisoners who had no involvement with narcotics. Concerning the royal family's own involvement in the drug trade, see p. 117, n. 167.

[14a] Imām Khomeini's complain is referring to another point; that is, the absence of justice. [Pub.]

12

woman be stoned[14b]), then they start wailing and lamenting: "What a harsh law that is, reflecting the harshness of the Arabs!" They are not aware that these penal provisions of Islam are intended to keep great nations from being destroyed by corruption. Sexual vice has now reached such proportions that it is destroying entire generations, corrupting our youth, and causing them to neglect all forms of work. They are all rushing to enjoy the various forms of vice that have become so freely available and so enthusiastically promoted. Why should it be regarded as harsh if Islam stipulates that an offender must be publicly flogged[14c] in order to protect the younger generation from corruption?

At the same time, we see the masters of this ruling class of ours enacting slaughters in Vietnam over fifteen years,[14d] devoting enormous budgets to this business of bloodshed, and no one has the right to object! But if Islam commands its followers to engage in warfare or defense in order to make men submit to laws that are beneficial for them, and kill a few corrupt people or instigators of corruption, then they ask: "What's the purpose for that war?"

All of the foregoing represent plans drawn up several centuries ago that are now being implemented and bearing fruit.

First, they opened a school in a certain place[174] and we overlooked the matter and said nothing. Our colleagues also were negligent in the matter and failed to prevent it from being established so that now, as you can observe, these schools have multiplied, and their missionaries have gone out into the provinces and villages, turning our children into Christians or unbelievers.

[14b] Under the penal laws of Islam, proof of the married status is one of the indispensable requisites for stoning an adulterer. Married man or woman is one who is mature (bāligh), mentally sound, and has a permanent spouse. [Pub.]

[14c] In Islamic law, the presence of a number of believers at the time of penal execution has been considered part of etiquettes of punishing the offender. Shī'ah jurists have been emphasizing on the observance of this tradition at the time of penal execution for adultery, slandering, and pandering. Their religious edict regarding the first case is based on Sūrah an-Nūr (24:2): "And a number of believers must witness the punishment of adulterer men and women." Another reason for it is that the attendants would take lesson from the requital, and anyone who is inclined to do so or is guilty of the same, would desist or cease from its performance. [Pub.]

[14d] After many years of resistance against the French and Japanese colonizers, in 1960 Vietnam had once again engaged in a protracted war with the United States. This war that ended in 1973 with the defeat and withdrawal of the American forces, brought untold destructions and casualties on the Vietnamese people. As the official figures fall short of exactly describing the degree of casualties and damages wrought by this ruthless aggression, the realities of the bitter contemporary history can be gleaned to some extent: Up to early 1965 when the scope of the war extended to South Vietnam, the number of South Vietnamese who perished or were injured is as follows: 170,000 died, 800,00 wounded, and 400,000 imprisoned. During that time the number of persons who had been sent on concentration camps, which are called "agricultural units" exceeds 5 millions. According to the *Voice of America* (January 6, 1963), throughout 1962 US Air Force had attacked 50 thousand times villages beyond the realm of "state villages," and based on the assertions of General Herkins(?), on the same year about 30 thousand villages perished. US Air Force operations in South Vietnam reached 30 thousand times a month. According to a news report of the *New York Times*, in a combined US and Saigon government air operations nearly 1,400 out of 2,600 villages in the South were totally ruined by napalm bombs and chemical weapons. A Red Cross report indicates that as the effect of using poisonous elements in the vast and populous areas, thousands of residents in the South have been afflicted with divergent diseases particularly skin-related ones and for a long time they have experienced sufferings and discomforts arising from the sickness. Moreover, many herds of cows and buffalos as well as other four-footed domesticated animals had died while leaves, flowers, and fruits of tree and rice fields were completely devastated. [Pub.]

[174] We have not been able to determine whether this is an allusion to a particular school established by foreigners. Before the Islamic Revolution, there were a number of foreign-run schools in Iran—secular and missionary—that in effect alienated their students from Islamic culture and society.

13

Their plan is to keep us backward, to keep us in our present miserable state so they can exploit our riches, our underground wealth, our lands, and our human resources. They want us to remain afflicted and wretched, and our poor to be trapped in their misery. Instead of surrendering to the injunctions of Islam, which provide a solution for the problem of poverty, they and their agents wish to go on living in huge places and enjoy lives of abominable luxury.

These plans of theirs are so broad in scope that they have even touched the institutions of religious learning. If someone wishes to speak about an Islamic government and the establishment of Islamic government, he must observe the principle of *taqiyyah*[175] and count upon the opposition of those who have sold themselves to imperialism. When this book was first printed, the agents of the embassy undertook certain desperate measures to prevent its dissemination,[176] which succeeded only in disgracing themselves more than before.

Matters have now come to the point where some people consider the apparel of a soldier incompatible with true manliness and justice, even though the leaders of our religion were all soldiers, commanders, and warriors. They put on military dress and went into battle in the wars that are described for us in our history; they killed and they were killed. The Commander of the Faithful[177] ('a) himself would place a helmet on his blessed head, don his coat of chain mail, and gird on a sword. Imām Hasan[178] and the Doyen of the Martyrs ('a), acted likewise. The later Imāms did not have the opportunity to go into battle, even though Imām Bāqir[179] ('a) was also a warrior by nature. But now the wearing of military apparel is thought to detract from a man's quality of justice,[180] and it is said that one should not wear military dress. If we want to form an Islamic government, then we must do it in our cloaks and turbans; otherwise, we commit an offense against decency and justice!

This is all the result of the wave of propaganda that has now reached the religious institution and imposed on us the duty of proving that Islam also possesses rules of government.

---

[175] *Taqiyyah*: prudential dissimulation of one's true beliefs under conditions of acute danger, a practice based on Qur'an, 3:28. For a fuller discussion of *taqiyyah*, see 'Allāmah Tabātabā'i, *Shi'ite Islam* (Albany, N.Y., 1975), pp. 223-225, *Al-Taqiyya Dissimulation*, and also p. 133 of the present work. [Pub.]

[176] This is a reference to an earlier and briefer series of talks given by Imām Khomeini on the subject of Islamic government. The Iranian embassy in Baghdad had sought to prevent the published text of those talks from being distributed.

[177] The Commander of the Faithful: 'Ali ibn Abi Tālib, cousin and son-in-law of the Prophet, and first of the Twelve Imāms from the Prophet's Progeny. He exercised rule from 35/656 until his martyrdom in 40/661. See Yousuf N. Lalljee, *'Ali the Magnificent* (Qum: Ansariyan Publications, 1987); Muhammad Jawād Chirri, *The Brother of the Prophet Mohammad (Imām 'Ali)*, (Qum: Ansariyan Publications); George Jordaq, *The Voice of Human Justice*, trans. M. Fazal Haq (Qum: Ansariyan Publications, 1990) [Pub.]

[178] Imām Hasan: son of Imām 'Ali and second of the Imāms. He was poisoned in 50/670 after spending most of his life in seclusion in Medina. See Shaykh Rādi Āl-Yāsīn, *Sulh al-Hasan: The Peace Treaty of Al-Hasan*, trans. Jāsim al-Rasheed (Qum: Ansariyan Publications, 1998),

[179] Imām Bāqir: the fifth Imām. He was born in 57/675 and spent most of his life in Medina, until his martydom there in 114/732. See Bāqir Sharīf al-Qarashi, *The Life of Imām Mohammed al-Bāqir*, trans. Jāsim al-Rasheed (Qum: Ansariyan Publications, 1999). [Pub.]

[180] The "quality of justice" that is demanded of a religious scholar includes not only the practice of equity in all social dealings, but also complete abstention from major sins, the consistent performance of all devotional duties, and the avoidance of conduct incompatible with decorum. Justice is among the requisites for becoming a judge, rector (*mufti*), and congregational prayer leader (*imām*). At the margin of the book, *Sharh-i Lum'ah*, vol. 1, chap. 11, p. 98, wearing of indecent clothes in the congregational prayers has been considered contrary to the spirit of magnanimity (*muruwwah*) and justice. [Pub.]

That is our situation then—created for us by the foreigners through their propaganda and their agents. They have removed from operation all the judicial processes and political laws of Islam and replaced them with European importations, thus diminishing the scope of Islam and ousting it from Islamic society. For the sake of exploitation they have installed their agents in power.

So far, we have sketched the subversive and corrupting plan of imperialism. We must now take into consideration as well certain internal factors notably the dazzling effect that the material progress of the imperialist countries has had on some members of our society. As the imperialist countries attained a high degree of wealth and affluence— the result both of scientific and technical progress and of their plunder of the nations of Asia and Africa—these individuals lost all their self-confidence and imagined that the only way to achieve technical progress was to abandon their own laws and beliefs. When the moon landings took place, for instance, they concluded that Muslims should jettison their laws! But what is the connection between going to the moon and the laws of Islam? Do they not see that countries having opposing laws and social systems compete with each other in technical and scientific progress and the conquest of space? Let them go all the way to Mars or beyond the Milky Way; they will still be deprived of true happiness, moral virtues and spiritual advancement and be unable to solve their own social problems. For the solution of social problems and the relief of human misery require foundations in faith and moral; merely acquiring material power and wealth, conquering nature and space, have no effect in this regard. They must be supplemented by, and balanced with, the faith, the conviction, and the morality of Islam in order truly to serve humanity instead of endangering it. This conviction, this morality, and these laws that are needed, we already possess. So, as soon as someone goes somewhere or invents something, we should not hurry to abandon our religion and its laws, which regulate the life of man and provide for his well being in this world and hereafter.

The same applies to the propaganda of the imperialists. Unfortunately some members of our society have been influenced by their hostile propaganda, although they should not have been. The imperialists have propagated among us the view that Islam does not have a specific form of government or governmental institutions. They say further that even if Islam does have certain laws, it has no method for enforcing them, so that its function is purely legislative. This kind of propaganda forms part of the overall plan of the imperialists to prevent the Muslims from becoming involved in political activity and establishing an Islamic government. It is in total contradiction with our fundamental beliefs.

We believe in government and believe that the Prophet (s) was bound to appoint a successor, as he indeed did.[21a] Was a successor designated purely for the sake of expounding law? The expounding of law did not require a successor to the Prophet. He himself, after all, had expounded the laws; it would have been enough for the laws to be written down in a book and put into people's hands to guide them in their actions. It was logically necessary for a successor to be appointed for the sake of exercising government. Law requires a person to execute it. The same holds true in all

---

[21a] The Most Noble Messenger (s) indicated in many instances the successorship of Imām 'Ali ibn Abi Tālib ('a) such as in Hadīth Yawm ad-Dār (Day of the Prophet's invitation to his kinsmen); Hadīth Manzilah (The Prophet's designation of 'Ali as his deputy in Medina during the Tabuk expedition); Āyat al-Wilāyah ('Ali's offering of a ring to a beggar and the subsequent revelation of a pertinent verse); Event of Ghadīr Khumm; and Hadīth ath-Thaqalayn. See Tafsir Kabīr, vol. 12, pp. 28, 53 under Sūrah al-Mā'idah, verses 55, 67; Sīrah ibn Hisham, vol. 4, p. 520; Tārīkh Tabari, vol. 2, pp. 319, 322; Al-Ghadīr, vols. 1-3; Caliphate of Imām 'Ali,

countries of the world, for the establishment of a law is of little benefit in itself and cannot secure the happiness of man. After a law is established, it is necessary also to create an executive power. If a system of law or government lacks an executive power, it is clearly deficient. Thus Islam, just as it established laws, also brought into being an executive power.

There was still a further question: who was to hold the executive power? If the Prophet (s) had not appointed a successor to assume the executive power, he would have failed to complete his mission, as the Qur'an testifies.[181] The necessity for the implementation of divine law, the need for an executive power, and the importance of that power in fulfilling the goals of the prophetic mission and establishing a just order that would result in the happiness of mankind—all of this made the appointment of a successor synonymous with the completion of the prophetic mission. In the time of the Prophet (s), laws were not merely expounded and promulgated; they were also implemented. The Messenger of God (s) was an executor of the law. For example, he implemented the penal provisions of Islam: he cut off the hand of the thief and administered lashings and stonings. The successor to the Prophet (s) must do the same; his task is not legislation, but the implementation of the divine laws that the Prophet (s) has promulgated. It is for this reason that the formation of a government and the establishment of executive organs are necessary. Belief in the necessity for these is part of the general belief in the Imamate, as are, too, exertion and struggle for the sake of establishing them.

Pay close attention. Whereas hostility toward you has led them to misrepresent Islam, it is necessary for you to present Islam and the doctrine of the Imamate correctly. You must tell people: "We believe in the Imamate; we believe that the Prophet (s), appointed a successor to assume responsibility for the affairs of the Muslims, and that he did so in conformity with the divine will. Therefore, we must also believe in the necessity for the establishment of government, and we must strive to establish organs for the execution of law and the administration of affairs." Write and publish books concerning the laws of Islam and their beneficial effects on society. Improve your style and method of preaching and related activity. *Know that it is your duty to establish an Islamic government.* Have confidence in yourselves and know that you are capable of fulfilling this task. The imperialists began laying their plans three or four centuries ago; they started out with nothing, but see where they are now! We too will begin with nothing, and we will pay no attention to the uproar created by a few "xenomaniacs"[182] and devoted servants of imperialism.

Present Islam to the people in its true form, so that our youth do not picture the *ākhūnds* as sitting in some corner in Najaf or Qum, studying the questions of menstruation and parturition instead of concerning themselves with politics, and draw the conclusion that religion must be separate from politics. This slogan of the separation of religion from politics and the demand that Islamic scholars should not

---

[181] "O Messenger! Proclaim what has been revealed to you by your Lord, for if you do not, you will not have fulfilled the mission He has entrusted to you" (4:67). On the commentary of this verse, see Mīr Ahmad 'Ali, *Text, Translation and Commentary of the Holy Qur'an* (Ehlmurst, NY: Tahrike Tarsile Qur'an, Inc., 1988),

[182] Xenomaniacs: those infatuated with foreign and especially Western models of culture. This is a translation of a Persian term, *gharbzādeh-ha*, popularized by Jalāl Āl-i Ahmad (d. 1969) in his book *Gharbzādegi* ("Xenomania"). See its English translation, R. Campbell (trans.) and Hamid Algar (ed. and anno.), *Occidentosis: A Plague from the West* (Berkeley: Al-Mizan Press, 1984). He was a writer of great influence and Imām Khomeini was acquainted with his work. See the commemorative supplement on Jalāl Āl-i Ahmad in the Tehran daily newspaper *Jumhūri-yi Islāmi*, Shahrīvar 20, 1359/October 12, 1980, p. 10. [Pub.]

intervene in social and political affairs have been formulated and propagated by the imperialists; it is only the irreligious who repeat them. Were religion and politics separate in the time of the Prophet (s)? Did there exist, on one side, a group of clerics, and opposite it, a group of politicians and leaders? Were religion and politics separate in the time of the caliphs—even if they were not legitimate—or in the time of the Commander of the Faithful ('a)? Did two separate authorities exist? These slogans and claims have been advanced by the imperialists and their political agents in order to prevent religion from ordering the affairs of this world and shaping Muslim society, and at the same time to create a rift between the scholars of Islam, on the one hand, and the masses and those struggling for freedom and independence, on the other. They will thus been able to gain dominance over our people and plunder our resources, for such has always been their ultimate goal.

If we Muslims do nothing but engage in the canonical prayer, petition God, and invoke His name, the imperialists and the oppressive governments allied with them will leave us alone. If we were to say "Let us concentrate on calling the *azān*[183] and saying our prayers. Let them come and rob us of everything we own—God will take care of them! There is no power or recourse except in Him, and God willing, we will be rewarded in the hereafter!"—if this were our logic, they would not disturb us.

Once during the occupation of Iraq, a certain British officer asked, " Is the *azān* I hear being called now on the minaret harmful to British policy?" When he was told that it was harmless, he said: "Then let him call for prayers as much as he wants!"

If you pay no attention to the policies of the imperialists, and consider Islam to be simply the few topics you are always studying and never go beyond them, then the imperialists will leave you alone. Pray as much as you like; it is your oil they are after—why should they worry about your prayers? They are after our minerals, and want to turn our country into a market for their goods. That is the reason the puppet governments they have installed prevent us from industrializing, and instead, establish only assembly plants and industry that is dependent on the outside world.

They do not want us to be true human beings, for they are afraid of true human beings. Even if only one true human being appears, they fear him, because others will follow him and he will have an impact that can destroy the whole foundation of tyranny, imperialism, and government by puppets. So, whenever some true human being has appeared they have either killed or imprisoned and exiled him, and tried to defame him by saying: "This is a political *ākhūnd*!" Now the Prophet (s) was also a political person. This evil propaganda is undertaken by the political agents of imperialism only to make you shun politics, to prevent you from intervening in the affairs of society and struggling against treacherous governments and their anti-national and anti-Islamic politics. They want to work their will as they please, with no one to bar their way.

---

[183] *Azān*: the call to prayer.

THE NECESSITY FOR
ISLAMIC GOVERNMENT

A BODY OF LAWS ALONE is not sufficient for a society to be reformed. In order for law to ensure the reform and happiness of man, there must be an executive power and an executor. For this reason, God Almighty, in addition to revealing a body of law (i.e., the ordinances of the *sharī'ah*), has laid down a particular form of government together with executive and administrative institution.

The Most Noble Messenger (s) headed the executive and administrative institutions of Muslim society. In addition to conveying the revelation and expounding and interpreting the articles of faith and the ordinances and institutions of Islam, he undertook the implementation of law and the establishment of the ordinances of Islam, thereby, bringing into being the Islamic state. He did not content himself with the promulgation of law; rather, he implemented it at the same time, cutting off hands and administering lashings, and stonings. After the Most Noble Messenger (s), his successor had the same duty and function. When the Prophet (s) appointed a successor, it was not only for the purpose of expounding articles of faith and law; it was for the implementation of law and the execution of God's ordinances. It was this function—the execution of law and the establishment of Islamic institutions—that made the appointment of a successor such an important matter that the Prophet (s) would have failed to fulfill his mission if he had neglected it. For after the Prophet (s), the Muslims still needed someone to execute laws and establish the institution of Islam in society, so that they might attain happiness in this world and the hereafter.

By their nature, in fact, laws and social institutions require the existence of an executor. It has always and everywhere been the case that legislation alone has little benefit: legislation by itself cannot assure the well-being of man. After the establishment of legislation, an executive power must come into being, a power that implements the laws and the verdicts given by the courts, thus allowing people to benefit from the laws and the just sentences the courts deliver. Islam has therefore established an executive power in the same way that it has brought laws into being. The person who holds this executive power is known as the *valī-yi amr*.[184]

The Sunnah[185] and path of the Prophet (s) constitute a proof of the necessity for establishing government. First, he himself established a government, as history testifies. He engaged in the implementation of laws, the establishment of the ordinances of Islam, and the administration of society. He sent out governors to different regions; both sat in judgment himself and also appointed judges; dispatched emissaries to foreign states, tribal chieftains, and kings; concluded treaties and pacts; and took command in battle. In short, he fulfilled all the functions of government. Second, he designated a ruler to succeed him, in accordance with divine command. If God Almighty, through the Prophet (s), designated a man who was to rule over Muslim society after him, this is in itself an indication that government remains a necessity after the departure of the Prophet from this world. Again, since the Most

---

[184] *Valī-yi Amr*: "the one who holds authority," a term derived from Qur'an, 4:59: "O you who believe! Obey God, and obey the Messenger and the holders of authority (*ūli 'l-amr*) from among you." For commentary of this verse, see Mīr Ahmad 'Ali, *The Holy Qur'an* (NY: Tahrike Tarsile Qur'an, 1988),

[185] Sunnah: the practice of the Prophet, accepted by Muslims as the norm and ideal for all human behavior.

Noble Messenger (s) promulgated the divine command through his act of appointing a successor, he also, implicitly stated the necessity for establishing a government.

It is self-evident that the necessity for enactment of the law, which necessitated the formation of a government by the Prophet (s), was confined or restricted to his time, but continues after his departure from this world. According to one of the noble verses of the Qur'an, the ordinances of Islam are not limited with respect to time or place; they are permanent and must be enacted until the end of time.[26a] They were not revealed merely for the time of the Prophet, only to be abandoned thereafter, with retribution and the penal code no longer be enacted, or the taxes prescribed by Islam no longer collected, and the defense of the lands and people of Islam suspended. The claim that the laws of Islam may remain in abeyance or are restricted to a particular time or place is contrary to the essential creedal bases of Islam. Since enactment of laws, then, is necessary after the departure of the Prophet from this world, and indeed, will remain so until the end of time, the formation of a government and the establishment of executive and administrative organs are also necessary. Without the formation of a government and the establishment of such organs to ensure that through enactment of the law, all activities of the individual take place in the framework of a just system, chaos and anarchy will prevail and social, intellectual and moral corruption will arise. The only way to prevent the emergence of anarchy and disorder and to protect society from corruption is to form a government and thus impart order to all the affairs of the country.

Both reason and divine law, then, demonstrate the necessity in our time for what was necessary during the lifetime of the Prophet (s) and the age of the Commander of the Faithful, 'Ali ibn Abi Talib ('a)—namely the formation of a government and the establishment of executive and administrative organs.

In order to clarify the matter further, let us pose the following question. From the time of the Lesser Occultation[186] down to the present (a period of more than twelve centuries that may continue for hundreds of millennia if it is not appropriate for the Occulted Imam to manifest himself), is it proper that the laws of Islam be cast aside and remain unexecuted, so that everyone acts as he pleases and anarchy prevails? Were the laws that the Prophet of Islam labored so hard for twenty-three years to set forth, promulgate, and execute valid only for a limited period of time? Was everything pertaining to Islam meant to be abandoned after the Lesser Occultation? Anyone who believes so, or voices such a belief, is worse situated than the person who believes and proclaims that Islam has been superseded or abrogated by another supposed revelation.[187]

[26a] See, for example, Sūrah Ibrāhīm (14:52), Sūrah Yūnus (10:2), Sūrah al-Hājj (22:49), Sūrah al-Ahzāb (33:40), and Sūrah Yā-Sīn (36:70). [Pub.]

[186] Lesser Occultation: *ghaybat-i sughrah*, the period of about 70 years (260/872-329/939) when, according to Shī'i belief, Muhammad al-Mahdi, the Twelfth Imam, absented himself from the physical plane but remained in communication with his followers through a succession of four appointed deputies, viz., 'Uthmān ibn Sa'īd, Muhammad ibn 'Uthmān, Husayn ibn Rūh, and 'Ali ibn Muhammad. At the death of the fourth deputies no successor was named, and the Greater Occultation (*ghaybat-i kubrah*) began, and continues to this day. See Muhammad Bāqir as-Sadr and Murtadā Mutahhari, *Awaited Saviour* (Karachi: Islamic Seminary Publications); Muhammad Bāqir as-Sadr, *An Inquiry Concerning Al-Mahdi* (Qum: Ansariyan Publications); Jassim M. Husain, *The Occultation of the Twelfth Imam: A Historical Background* (London: Muhammadi Trust, 1982); Ibrāhīm Amīni, *Al-Imām Al-Mahdī: The Just Leader of Humanity*, trans. 'Abdul 'Azīz Sachedina (Qum: Ansariyan Publications).

[187] The allusion is probably to the Bahā'is, who claim to have received a succession of post-Qur'anic revelations.

No one can say it is no longer necessary to defend the frontiers and the territorial integrity of the Islamic homeland; that taxes such as the *jizyah, kharāj, khums,* and *zakāt*[188] should no longer be collected; that the penal code of Islam, with its provisions for the payment of blood money and the exacting of requital, should be suspended. Any person who claims that the formation of an Islamic government is not necessary implicitly denies the necessity for the implementation of Islamic law, the universality and comprehensiveness of that law, and the eternal validity of the faith itself.

After the death of the Most Noble Messenger (s), none of the Muslims doubted the necessity for government. No one said: "We no longer need a government". No one was heard to say anything of the kind. There was unanimous agreement concerning the necessity for government. There was disagreement only as to which person should assume responsibility for government and head the state. Government, therefore, was established after the Prophet (s), both in the time of the caliphs and in that of the Commander of the Faithful ('a); an apparatus of government came into existence with administrative and executive organs.

The nature and character of Islamic law and the divine ordinances of the *sharī'ah* furnish additional proof of the necessity for establishing government, for they indicate that the laws were laid down for the purpose of creating a state and administering the political, economic and cultural affairs of society.

Firstly, the laws of the *sharī'ah* embrace a diverse body of laws and regulation, which amounts to a complete social system. In this system of laws, all the needs of man have been met: his dealings with his neighbors, fellow citizens, and clan, as well as children and relatives; the concerns of private and marital life; regulations concerning war and peace and intercourse with other nations; penal and commercial law; and regulations pertaining to trade, industry and agriculture. Islamic law contains provisions relating to the preliminaries of marriage and the form in which it should be contracted, and others relating to the development of the embryo in the womb, and what food the parents should eat at the time of conception. It further stipulates the duties that are incumbent upon them while the infant is being suckled, and specifies how the child should be reared, and how the husband and the wife should relate to each other and to their children. Islam provides laws and instructions for all of these matters, aiming, as it does, to produce integrated and virtuous human beings who are walking embodiments of the law, or to put it differently, the law's voluntary and instinctive executors. It is obvious, then, how much care Islam devotes to government and the political and economic relations of society, with goal of creating conditions conducive to the production of morally upright and virtuous human beings.

The Glorious Qur'an and the Sunnah contain all the laws and ordinances man needs in order to attain happiness and the perfection of his state. The book *al-Kāfi*[189] has a chapter entitled, "All the Needs of Men Are Set Out in the Book and the Sunnah,"[30a] the "Book" meaning the Qur'an, which is, in its own words, "an exposition of all

---

[188] *Jizyah:* a tax levied on non-Muslim citizens of the Muslim state in exchange for the protection they receive and in lieu of the taxes, such as *zakāt,* that only Muslims pay. *Kharaj:* a tax levied on certain categories of land. *Khums:* a tax consisting of one-fifth of agricultural and commercial profits (see p. 24 and Sayyid Muhammad Rizvi, *Khums*). *Zakāt:* the tax levied on various categories of wealth and spent on the purposes specified in Qur'an, 9:60. [Pub.]

[189] *Al-Kāfi:* more fully, *Al-Kāfi fī 'l Hadīth,* one of the most important Shī'i collections of *hadīth,* compiled by Shaykh Abū Ja'far Muhammad ibn Ya'qūb al-Kulayni (d. 329/941). This treatise consists of 34 books, 326 sections, and over 16,000 *ahādīth.* Two fascicules of this work have been translated into English by Sayyid Muhammad Hasan Rizvi and published by the Tehran-based World Organization for Islamic Services (WOFIS).

[30a] *Usūl al-Kāfi,* Book of "Virtues of Knowledge," vol. 1, pp. 76-80. [Pub.]

things."[190] According to certain traditions, the Imām[191] also swears that the Book and the Sunnah contain without a doubt all that men need.

Second, if we examine closely the nature and character of the provisions of the law, we realize that their execution and implementation depend upon the formation of a government, and that it is impossible to fulfill the duty of executing God's commands without there being established properly comprehensive administrative and executive organs. Let us now mention certain types of provisions in order to illustrate this point; the others you can examine yourselves.

The taxes Islam levies and the form of budget it has established are not merely for the sake of providing subsistence to the poor or feeding the indigent among the descendants of the Prophet (s); they are also intended to make possible, the establishment of a great government and to assure its essential expenditures.

For example, *khums* is a huge source of income that accrues to the treasury and represents one item in the budget. According to our Shī'i school of thought, *khums* is to be levied in an equitable manner on all agricultural and commercial profits and all natural resources whether above or below the ground—in short, on all forms of wealth and income. It applies equally to the greengrocer with his stall outside this mosque, and to the shipping or mining magnate. They must all pay one-fifth of their surplus income, after customary expenses are deducted, to the Islamic ruler, so that it enters the treasury. It is obvious that such a huge income serves the purpose of administering the Islamic state and meeting all its financial needs. If we were to calculate one-fifth of the surplus income of all the Muslim countries (or of the whole world, should it enter the fold of Islam), it would become fully apparent that the purpose for the imposition of such a tax is not merely the upkeep of the *sayyids*[192] or the religious scholars, but on the contrary, something far more significant—namely, meeting the financial needs of the great organs and institutions of government. If an Islamic government is achieved, it will have to be administered on the basis of the taxes that Islam has established—*khums*, *zakāt* (this, of course, would not represent an appreciable sum)[193] *jizyah*, and *kharāj*.

How could the *sayyids* ever need so vast a budget? The *khums* of the bazaar of Baghdad would be enough for the needs of the *sayyids* and the upkeep of the religious teaching institution, as well as all the poor of the Islamic world, quite apart from the *khums* of the bazaars of Tehran, Istanbul, Cairo, and other cities. The provision of such a huge budget must obviously be for the purpose of forming a government and administering the Islamic lands. It was established with the aim of providing for the needs of the people, for public services relating to health, education, defense, and economic development. Further, in accordance with the procedures laid down by Islam for the collection, preservation, and expenditure of this income, all forms of usurpation and embezzlement of public wealth have been forbidden; so that the head of state and all those entrusted with responsibility for conducting public affairs (i.e., members of the government) have no privileges over the ordinary citizen in benefiting from the public income and wealth; all have an equal share.

---

[190] Qur'an, 16:89.

[191] The reference is probably to Imām Ja'far as-Sādiq, whose sayings on this subject are quoted by 'Allāmah Tabātabā'i in *al-Mīzān fī Tafsīr al-Qur'ān* (Beirut, 1390/1979), XII, 327-328. First eight volumes of 'Allāmah Tabātabā'i's *Al-Mīzān* has been translated into English by Sayyid Saeed Akhtar Rizvi and published by the WOFIS. [Pub.]

[192] *Sayyids*: the descendants of the Prophet through his daughter Fātimah and son-in-law 'Ali, the first of the Twelve Imāms.

[193] *Zakāt* would not represent an appreciable sum presumably because it is levied on surplus wealth, the accumulation of which is inhibited by the economic system of Islam.

Now, should we cast this huge treasury into the ocean, or bury it until the Imām returns, or just spend it on fifty *sayyids* a day until they have all eaten their fill? Let us suppose we give all this money to 500,000 *sayyids*; they would not know what to do with it. We all know that the *sayyids* and the poor have a claim on the public treasury only to the extent required for subsistence. The budget of the Islamic state is constructed in such a way that every source of income is allocated to specific types of expenditures. *Zakāt*, voluntary contributions and charitable donations, and *khums* are all levied and spent separately. There is a *hadīth* to the effect that at the end of the year, *sayyids* must return any surplus from what they have received to the Islamic ruler, just as the ruler must aid them if they are in need.

The *jizyah*, which is imposed on the *ahl adh-dhimmah*,[194] and the *kharāj*, which is levied on agricultural land, represent two additional sources of considerable income. The establishment of these taxes also proves that the existence of a ruler and a government is necessary. It is the duty of a ruler or governor to assess the poll tax to be levied on the *ahl adh-dhimmah* in accordance with their income and financial capacity, and to fix appropriate taxes on their arable lands and livestock. He must also collect the *kharāj* on those broad lands that are the "property of God" and in the possession of the Islamic state. This task requires the existence of orderly institutions, rules and regulations, and administrative procedures and policies; it cannot be fulfilled in the absence of order. It is the responsibility of those in charge of the Islamic state, first, to assess the taxes in due and appropriate measure and in accordance with the public good; then, to collect them; and finally, to spend them in a manner conducive to the welfare of the Muslims.

Thus, you see that the fiscal provisions of Islam also point to the necessity for establishing a government, for they cannot be fulfilled without the establishment of the appropriate Islamic institutions.

The ordinances pertaining to preservation of the Islamic system and defense of the territorial integrity and independence of the Islamic *ummah*[195] also demanded the formation of a government. An example is the command: "Prepare against them whatever force you can muster and horses tethered" (Qur'an, 8:60), which enjoins the preparation of as much armed defensive force as possible and orders the Muslims to be always on the alert and at the ready, even in time of peace.

If the Muslims had acted in accordance with this command, and after forming a government, made the necessary extensive preparations to be in a state of full readiness for war, a handful of Jews would never have dared to occupy our lands and to burn and destroy the Masjid al-Aqsā[196] without the people's being capable of making an immediate response. All this has resulted from the failure of the Muslims to fulfill their duty of executing God's law and setting up a righteous and respectable government. If the rulers of the Muslim countries truly represented the believers and enacted God's ordinances, they would set aside their petty differences, abandon their subversive and divisive activities, and join together like the fingers of one hand. Then a handful of wretched Jews (the agents of America, Britain and other foreign powers) would never have been able to accomplish what they have, no matter how much

---

[194] *Ahl adh-Dhimmah*: non-Muslim citizens of the Muslim state, whose rights and obligations are contractually determined.

[195] *Ummah*: the entire Islamic community, without territorial or ethnic distinction.

[196] Masjid al-Aqsā: the site in Jerusalem where the Prophet ascended to heaven in the eleventh year of his mission (Qur'an, 17:1); also the complex of mosques and buildings erected on the site. The chief of these was extensively damaged by arson in 1969, two years after the Zionist usurpation of Jerusalem.

support they enjoyed from America and Britain. All this has happened because of the incompetence of those who rule over the Muslims.

The verse: "Prepare against them whatever force you can muster" commands you to be as strong and well-prepared as possible, so that your enemies will be unable to oppress you and transgress against you. It is because we have been lacking in unity, strength, and preparedness that we suffer oppression and are at the mercy of foreign aggressors.

There are numerous provisions of the law that cannot be implemented without the establishment of a government apparatus; for example, blood money, which must be exacted and delivered to those deserving it, or the corporeal penalties imposed by the law, which must be carried out under the supervision of the Islamic ruler. All of these laws refer back to the institutions of government for it is the government power alone that is capable of fulfilling this function.

After the death of the Most Noble Messenger (s), the obstinate enemies of the faith, the Umayyads[197] (God's curses be upon them), did not permit the Islamic state to attain stability with the rule of 'Ali ibn Abi Talib ('a). They did not allow a form of government to exist that was pleasing to God, Exalted and Almighty, and to His Most Noble Messenger (s). They transformed the entire basis of government, and their policies were, for the most part, contradictory to Islam. The form of government of the Umayyads and the Abbasids,[198] and the political and administrative policies they pursued, were anti-Islamic. The form of government was thoroughly perverted by being transformed into a monarchy, like those of the kings of Iran, the emperors of Rome, and the pharaohs of Egypt. For the most part, this non-Islamic form of government has persisted to the present day, as we can see.

Both law and reason require that we not permit governments to retain this non-Islamic or anti-Islamic character. The proofs are clear. First, the existence of a non-Islamic political order necessarily results in the non-implementation of the Islamic political order. Then, all non-Islamic systems of government are the systems of $kufr$[199] since the ruler in each case is an instance of $t\bar{a}gh\bar{u}t$,[200] and it is our duty to remove from the life of Muslim society all traces of $kufr$ and destroy them. It is also our duty to create a favorable social environment for the education of believing and virtuous individuals, an environment that is in total contradiction with that produced by the rule of $t\bar{a}gh\bar{u}t$ and illegitimate power. The social environment created by $t\bar{a}gh\bar{u}t$ and $shirk$[201] invariably brings about corruption such as you can observe now in Iran, the same corruption termed "corruption on earth."[202] This corruption must be swept away, and

---

[197] Umayyads: descendants of 'Umayyah ibn 'Abdu Shams ibn 'Abdu Manāf from the Quraysh tribe, and members of the dynasty that ruled at Damascus from 41/632 until 132/750 and transformed the caliphate into a hereditary institution. Mu'āwiyah, ibn Abū Sufyān frequently mentioned in these pages, was the first of the Umayyad line. This kingdom ended with the murder of Marwān II, the last Umayyad caliph. [Pub.]

[198] Abbasids: offspring of 'Abbās ibn 'Abdul Muttalib, uncle of the Holy Prophet (s), and the dynasty that replaced the Umayyads and established a new caliphal capital in Baghdad. This dynastic rule began in 132/750 with the caliphate of 'Abdullāh as-Saffāh. With the rise of various local rulers, generally of military origin, the power of the Abbasids began to decline from the fourth/tenth century and it was brought to an end by the Mongol conquest in 656/1258. [Pub.]

[199] $Kufr$: the rejection of divine guidance; the antithesis of Islam.

[200] $T\bar{a}gh\bar{u}t$: one who surpasses all bounds in his despotism and tyranny and claims the prerogatives of divinity for himself, whether explicitly or implicitly. See also p. 78-79.

[201] $Shirk$: the assignment of partners to God, either by believing in a multiplicity of gods, or by assigning divine attributes and prerogatives to other-than-God.

[202] "Corruption on earth": a broad term including not only moral corruption, but also subversion of the public good, embezzlement and usurpation of public wealth, conspiring with the enemies of the

its instigators should be punished for their deeds. It is the same corruption that the Pharaoh generated in Egypt with his policies, so that the Qur'an says of him, "Truly, he was among the corruptors" (28:4). A believing, pious, just individual cannot possibly exist in a socio-political environment of this nature, and still maintain his faith and righteous conduct. He is faced with two choices: either he commits acts that amount to *kufr* and contradict righteousness, or in order not to commit such acts and not to submit to the orders and commands of *tāghūt*, the just individual opposes him and struggles against him in order to destroy the environment of corruption. We have in reality, then, no choice but to destroy those systems of government that are corrupt in themselves and also entail the corruption of others, and to overthrow all treacherous, corrupt, oppressive, and criminal regimes.

This is a duty that all Muslims must fulfill, in every one of the Muslim countries, in order to achieve the triumphant political revolution of Islam.

We see, too, that together, the imperialists and the tyrannical self-seeking rulers have divided the Islamic homeland. They have separated the various segments of the Islamic *ummah* from each other and artificially created separate nations. There once existed the great Ottoman State, and that, too, the imperialists divided. Russia, Britain, Austria, and other imperialist powers united, and through wars against the Ottomans, each came to occupy or absorb into its sphere of influence, part of the Ottoman realm. It is true that most of the Ottoman rulers were incompetent, that some of them were corrupt, and that they followed the monarchical system. Nonetheless, the existence of the Ottoman State represented a threat to the imperialists. It was always possible that righteous individuals *might* rise up among the people and, with their assistance, seize control of the state, thus putting an end to imperialism by mobilizing the unified resources of the nation. Therefore after numerous prior wars, the imperialists at the end of World War I divided the Ottoman State, creating in its territories about ten or fifteen petty states.[203] Then each of these was entrusted to one of their servants or a group of their servants, although certain countries were later able to escape the grasp of the agents of imperialism.

In order to assure the unity of the Islamic *ummah*, in order to liberate the Islamic homeland from occupation and penetration by the imperialists and their puppet governments, it is imperative that we establish a government. In order to attain the unity and freedom of the Muslim peoples, we must overthrow the oppressive governments installed by the imperialists and bring into existence an Islamic government of justice that will be in the service of the people. The formation of such a government will serve to preserve the disciplined unity of the Muslims; just as Fāṭimah az-Zahrā[204] ('a) said in her address: "The Imamate exists for the sake of preserving order among the Muslims and replacing their disunity with unity".

Through the political agents they have placed in power over the people, the imperialists have imposed on us an unjust economic order, and thereby divided our

---

community against its security, and working in general for the overthrow of the Islamic order. See the commentary on Qur'an, 5:33 in Ṭabāṭabā'i's, *al-Mīzān*, V, 330-332.

[203] It may be apposite to quote here the following passage from a secret report drawn up in January 1916 by Thomas E. Lawrence, the British organizer of the so-called Arab revolt led by Sharīf Husayn of Mecca: "Husayn's activity seems beneficial to us, because it matches with our immediate aims, the breakup of the Islamic bloc and the defeat and disruption of the Ottoman Empire.... The Arabs are even less stable than the Turks. If properly handled they would remain in a state of political mosaic, a tissue of small jealous principalities incapable of political cohesion." See Philip Knightley and Colin Simpson, *The Secret Lives of Lawrence of Arabia* (New York, 1971), p. 55.

[204] Fāṭimah az-Zahrā: Fāṭimah, the daughter of the Prophet and wife of Imām 'Ali. For her biography, see *Fāṭimah the Gracious* (Qum: Ansariyan Publications). [Pub.]

24

people into two groups: oppressors and oppressed. Hundreds of millions of Muslims are hungry and deprived of all forms of health care and education, while minorities comprised of the wealthy and powerful live a life of indulgence, licentiousness, and corruption. The hungry and deprived have constantly struggled to free themselves from the oppression of their plundering overlords, and their struggle continues to this day. But their way is blocked by the ruling minorities and the oppressive governmental structures they head. It is our duty to save the oppressed and deprived. It is our duty to be a helper to the oppressed, and an enemy to the oppressor. This is nothing other than the duty that the Commander of the Faithful ('a) entrusted to his two great offspring[205] in his celebrated testament: "Be an enemy to the oppressor and a helper to the oppressed."[46a]

The scholars of Islam have a duty to struggle against all attempts by oppressors to establish a monopoly over the sources of wealth or to make illicit use of them. They must not allow the masses to remain hungry and deprived while plundering oppressors usurp the sources of wealth and live in opulence. The Commander of the Faithful ('a) says: "I have accepted the task of government because God, Exalted and Almighty, has exacted from the scholars of Islam a pledge not to sit silent and idle in the face of gluttony and plundering of the oppressors, on the one hand, and the hunger and deprivation of the oppressed, on the other." Here is the full text of the passage we refer to:

> "I swear by Him Who causes the seed to open and creates the souls of all living things that were it not for the presence of those who have come to swear allegiance to me, were it not for the obligation of rulership now imposed upon me by the availability of aid and support, and were it not for the pledge that God has taken from the scholars of Islam not to remain silent in the face of the gluttony and plundering of the oppressors, on the one hand, and the harrowing hunger and deprivation of the oppressed, on the other hand---were it not for all of this, then I would abandon the reins of government and in no way seek it. You would see that this world of yours, with all of its position and rank, is less in my eyes than the moisture that comes from the sneeze of a goat."[206]

How can we stay silent and idle today when we see that a band of traitors and usurpers, the agents of foreign powers, have appropriated the wealth and the fruits of labor of hundreds of millions of Muslims—thanks to the support of their masters and through the power of the bayonet—granting the Muslim not the least right to prosperity? It is the duty of Islamic scholars and all Muslims to put an end to this system of oppression and, for the sake of the well-being of hundreds of millions of human beings, to overthrow these oppressive governments and form an Islamic government.

Reason, the laws of Islam, and the practice of the Prophet (s), and that of the Commander of the Faithful ('a), the purport of various Qur'anic verses and Prophetic traditions—all indicate the necessity of forming a government. As an example of the traditions of the Imāms, I now quote the following tradition of Imām Ridā[207] ('a):

---

[205] I.e., Hasan and Husayn.
[46a] *Nahj al-Balāghah*, Letter 47. See English translation of *Nahj al-Balāghah, Peak of Eloquence* with commentary and its original Arabic text (Qum: Ansariyan Publications).
[206] *Nahj al-Balāghah*, Sermon 3 (The famous *Shaqshaqiyyah* Sermon). See *Nahj al-Balāghah*, ed. Subhi as-Sālih. [Pub.]
[207] Imām Ridā: eighth of the Twelve Imāms, born in 148/765 and died in 203/817 in Tūs (Mashhad). He was poisoned by the Abbasid caliph Ma'mūn, who had appointed him as his successor at first, but then grew fearful of the wide following he commanded (see p. 137). His shrine in Mashhad is one of the principal centers of pilgrimage and religious learning in Iran. See Bāqir Sharīf al-Qarashi, *The Life*

'Abd al-Wāhid ibn Muhammad ibn 'Abdus an-Neyshābūri al-'Attār said: "I was told by Abū 'l-Hasan 'Ali ibn Muhammad ibn Qutayba an-Neyshābūri that he was told by Abū Muhammad al-Fadl ibn Shadhan an-Neyshābūri this tradition. If someone asks, 'Why has God, the All-Wise, appointed the holders of authority and commanded us to obey them?' then we answer, 'For numerous reasons. One reason is this: Men are commanded to observe certain limits and not to transgress them in order to avoid the corruption that would result. This cannot be attained or established without there being appointed over them a trustee who will ensure that they remain within the limits of the licit and prevent them from casting themselves into the danger of transgression. Were it not for such a trustee, no one would abandon his own pleasure and benefit because of the corruption it might entail for another. Another reason is that we find no group or nation of men that ever existed without a ruler and leader, since it is required by both religion and worldly interest. It would not be compatible with divine wisdom to leave mankind to its own devices, for He, the All-Wise, knows that men need a ruler for their survival. It is through the leadership he provides that men make war against their enemies, divide among themselves the spoils of war, and preserve their communal solidarity, preventing the oppression of the oppressed by the oppressor.

" 'A further reason is this: were God not to appoint over men a solicitous, trustworthy, protecting, reliable leader, the community would decline, religion would depart, and the norms and ordinances that have been revealed would undergo change. Innovators would increase and deniers would erode religion, inducing doubt in the Muslims. For we see that men are needy and defective, judging by their differences of opinion and inclination and their diversity of state. Were a trustee, then, not appointed to preserve what has been revealed through the Prophet (s), corruption would ensue in the manner we have described. Revealed laws, norms, ordinances, and faith would be altogether changed, and therein would lie the corruption of all mankind.' "[208]

We have omitted the first part of the *hadīth*, which pertains to prophethood, a topic not germane to our present discussion. What interests us at present is the second half, which I will now paraphrase for you.

If someone should ask you, "Why has God, the All-Wise, appointed holders of authority and commanded you to obey them?" you should answer him as follows: "He has done so for various causes and reasons. One is that men have been set upon a certain well- defined path, and commanded not to stray from it, nor to transgress against the established limits and norms, for if they were to stray, they would fall prey to corruption. Now men would not be able to keep to their ordained path and to enact God's laws unless a trustworthy and protective individual (or power) were appointed over them with responsibility for this matter, to prevent them from stepping outside the sphere of the licit and transgressing against the rights of others. If no such restraining individual or power were appointed, nobody would voluntarily abandon any pleasure or interest of his own that might result in harm or corruption to others; everybody would engage in oppressing and harming others for the sake of his own pleasures and interests.

"Another reason and cause is this: we do not see a single group, nation, or religious community that has ever been able to exist without an individual entrusted with the maintenance of its laws and institutions—in short, a head or a leader; for such a person is essential for fulfilling the affairs of religion and the world. It is not permissible, therefore, according to divine wisdom that God should leave men, His creatures, without a leader and guide, for He knows well that they depend on the

of Imām 'Ali bin Mūsā al-Ridā, trans. Jāsim al-Rasheed (Qum: Ansariyan Publications); Muhammad Jawād Fadlallāh, *Imam al-Ridā: A Historical and Biographical Research*, trans. Yāsīn T. al-Jibouri; Muhammad Mahdi Shams ad-Dīn, "Al-Imām ar-Ridā ('a).
[208] The text of this tradition can be found in Shaykh Sadūq, *'Ilal ash-Sharāi'* (Qum, 1378/1958), I, sec. 182, *hadīth* 9, p. 251. [Pub.]

existence of such a person for their own survival and perpetuation. It is under his leadership that they fight against their enemies, divide the public income among themselves, perform Friday and other congregational prayers and foreshorten the arms of the transgressors who would encroach on the rights of the oppressed.

"Another proof and cause is this: were God not to appoint an Imām over men to maintain law and order, to serve the people faithfully as a vigilant trustee, religion would fall victim to obsolescence and decay. Its rites and institutions would vanish; the customs and ordinances of Islam would be transformed or even deformed. Heretical innovators would add things to religion and atheists and unbelievers would subtract things from it, presenting it to the Muslims in an inaccurate manner. For we see that men are prey to defects; they are not perfect, and must need to strive for perfection. Moreover, they disagree with each other, having varying inclinations and discordant states. If God, therefore, had not appointed over men one who would maintain order and law and protect the revelation brought by the Prophet (s), in the manner we have described, men would have fallen prey to corruption; the institutions, laws, customs, and ordinances of Islam would be transformed; and faith and its content would be completely changed, resulting in the corruption of all humanity."

As you can deduce from the words of the Imām ('a), there are numerous proofs and causes that necessitate formation of a government, and establishment of an authority. These proofs, causes, and arguments are not temporary in their validity or limited to a particular time, and the necessity for the formation of a government, therefore, is perpetual. For example, it will always happen that men overstep the limits laid down by Islam and transgress against the rights of others for the sake of their personal pleasure and benefit. It cannot be asserted that such was the case only in the time of the Commander of the Faithful ('a), and that afterwards, men became angels. The wisdom of the Creator has decreed that men should live in accordance with justice and act within the limits set by divine law. This wisdom is eternal and immutable, and constitutes one of the norms of God Almighty. Today and always, therefore, the existence of a holder of authority, a ruler who acts as trustee and maintains the institutions and laws of Islam, is a necessity—a ruler who prevents cruelty, oppression, and violation of the rights of others; who is a trustworthy and vigilant guardian of God's creatures; who guides men to the teachings, doctrines, laws, and institutions of Islam; and who prevents the undesirable changes that atheists and the enemies of religion wish to introduce in the laws and institutions of Islam. Did not the caliphate of the Commander of the Faithful ('a) serve this purpose? The same factors of necessity that led him to become the Imām still exist; the only difference is that no single individual has been designated for the task.[209] The principle of the necessity of government has been made a general one, so that it will always remain in effect.

If the ordinances of Islam are to remain in effect, then, if encroachment by oppressive ruling classes on the rights of the weak is to be prevented, if ruling minorities are not to be permitted to plunder and corrupt the people for the sake of pleasure and material interest, if the Islamic order is to be preserved and all individuals are to pursue the just path of Islam without any deviation, if innovations and the approval of anti-Islamic laws by sham parliaments[210] are to be prevented, if

---

[209] That is, in the absence of the Imām or an individual deputy named by him (as was the case during the Lesser Occultation), the task devolves upon the *fuqahā* as a class. See argument on pp. 44-112.

[210] Here the allusion may be in particular to the so-called Family Protection Law of 1967, which Imām Khomeini denounced as contrary to Islam in an important ruling. See Imām Khomeini, *Tauzih al-Masā'il*, n.p., n.d., pp. 462-463, par. 2836, and p. 441.

the influence of foreign powers in the Islamic lands is to be destroyed—government is necessary. None of these aims can be achieved without government and the organs of the state. It is a righteous government, of course, that is needed; one presided over by a ruler who will be a trustworthy and righteous trustee. Those who presently govern us are of no use at all for they are tyrannical, corrupt, and highly incompetent.

In the past, we did not act in concert and unanimity in order to establish proper government and overthrow treacherous and corrupt rulers. Some people were apathetic and reluctant even to discuss the theory of Islamic government, and some went so far as to praise oppressive rulers. It is for this reason that we find ourselves in the present state. The influence and sovereignty of Islam in society have declined; the nation of Islam has fallen victim to division and weakness; the laws of Islam have remained in abeyance and been subjected to change and modification; and the imperialists have propagated foreign laws and alien culture among the Muslims through their agents for the sake of their evil purposes, causing people to be infatuated with the West. It was our lack of a leader, a guardian, and our lack of institutions of leadership that made all this possible. We need righteous and proper organs of government; that much is self-evident.

THE FORM OF
ISLAMIC GOVERNMENT

ISLAMIC GOVERNMENT does not correspond to any of the existing forms of government. For example, it is not a tyranny, where the head of state can deal arbitrarily with the property and lives of the people, making use of them as he wills, putting to death anyone he wishes, and enriching anyone he wishes by granting landed estates and distributing the property and holdings of the people. The Most Noble Messenger (s), the Commander of the Faithful ('a), and the other caliphs did not have such powers. Islamic government is neither tyrannical nor absolute, but constitutional. It is not constitutional in the current sense of the word, i.e., based on the approval of laws in accordance with the opinion of the majority. It is constitutional in the sense that the rulers are subject to a certain set of conditions in governing and administering the country, conditions that are set forth in the Noble Qur'an and the Sunnah of the Most Noble Messenger (s). It is the laws and ordinances of Islam comprising this set of conditions that must be observed and practiced. Islamic government may therefore be defined as the rule of divine law over men.

The fundamental difference between Islamic government, on the one hand, and constitutional monarchies and republics, on the other, is this: whereas the representatives of the people or the monarch in such regimes engage in legislation, in Islam the legislative power and competence to establish laws belongs exclusively to God Almighty. The Sacred Legislator of Islam is the sole legislative power. No one has the right to legislate and no law may be executed except the law of the Divine Legislator. It is for this reason that in an Islamic government, a simple planning body takes the place of the legislative assembly that is one of the three branches of government. This body draws up programs for the different ministries in the light of the ordinances of Islam and thereby determines how public services are to be provided across the country.

The body of Islamic laws that exist in the Qur'an and Sunnah   has been accepted by the Muslims and recognized by them as worthy of obedience. This consent and acceptance facilitates the task of government and makes it truly belong to the people. In contrast, in a republic or a constitutional monarchy, most of those claiming to be representatives of the majority of people approve anything they wish as law and then impose it on the entire population.

Islamic government is a government of law. In this form of government, sovereignty belongs to God alone and law is His decree and command. The law of Islam, divine command, has absolute authority over all individuals and the Islamic government. Everyone, including the Most Noble Messenger (s) and his successors, is subject to law and will remain so for all eternity—the law that has been revealed by God, Almighty and Exalted, and expounded by the tongue of the Qur'an and the Most Noble Messenger (s). If the Prophet   (s) assumed the task of divine viceregency upon earth, it was in accordance with divine command. God, Almighty and Exalted, appointed him as His viceregent, "the viceregent of God upon earth"; he did not establish a government on his own initiative in order to be leader of the Muslims. Similarly, when it became apparent that disagreements would probably arise among the Muslims because their acquaintance with the faith was recent and limited, God Almighty charged the Prophet   (s), by way of revelation, to clarify the question of succession immediately, there in the middle of the desert. Then the Most Noble Messenger (s), nominated the Commander of the Faithful ('a) as his successor, in conformity and obedience to the law, not because he was his own son-in-law or had performed certain services, but because, he was acting in obedience to God's law, as its executor.[211]

In Islam, then, government has the sense of adherence to law; it is law alone that rules over society. Even the limited powers given to the Most Noble Messenger (s) and those exercising rule after him have been conferred upon them by God. Whenever the Prophet (s) expounded a certain matter or promulgated a certain injunction, he did so in obedience to divine law, a law that everyone without exception must obey and adhere to. Divine law obtains both for the leader and the led; the sole law that is valid and imperative to apply is the law of God. Obedience to the Prophet (s) also takes place in accordance with divine decree, for God says: "And obey the Messenger"(Qur'an, 4:59). Obedience to those entrusted with authority is also on the basis of divine decree: "And obey the holders of authority from among you"(Qur'an, 4:59). Individual opinion, even if it be that of the Prophet (s) himself, cannot intervene in matters of divine law; here, all are subject to the will of God.

Islamic government is not a form of monarchy, especially not an imperial one. In that type of government, the rulers are empowered over the property and persons of those they rule and may dispose of them entirely as they wish. Islam has not the slightest connection with this form and method of government. For this reason, we find that in Islamic government, unlike monarchial and imperial regimes, there is not the slightest trace of vast palaces, opulent buildings, servants and retainers, private equerries, adjutants to the heir apparent, and all the other appurtenances of monarchy that consume as much as half of the national budget. You all know how the Prophet (s) lived, the Prophet who was the head of the Islamic state and its ruler. The same mode of life was preserved until the beginning of the Umayyad period. The first two [caliphs] adhered to the Prophet's (s) example in the outer conduct of their personal lives, even though in other affairs they acted to the contrary, which led to the grave deviations that appeared in the time of 'Uthmān, the same deviations that have inflicted on us these misfortunes of the present day.[212] In the time of the Commander of the Faithful ('a), the system of government was corrected and a proper form and method of rule were followed. Even though that excellent man ruled over a vast realm that included Iran, Egypt, Hijāz[213] and the Yemen among its provinces, he lived more frugally than the most impoverished of our clergy students. According to tradition, he once bought two tunics, and finding one of them better than the other, he gave the better one to his servant Qanbar. The other he kept for himself, and since its sleeves were too long for him, he tore off the extra portion.[54a] In this torn garment, the ruler of a great, populous, and prosperous realm clothed himself.

---

[211] It is referring to the Prophet's appointment of Imām 'Ali as his successor at a gathering near the pool of Khumm during his return to Medina from Mecca, after having performed the last pilgrimage in his life. See Muhammad Bāqir as-Sadr, *Ghadīr* (Qum: Ansariyan Publications).

[212] The attribution of errors to Abū Bakr and 'Umar and deviations to 'Uthmān is a part of Shī'i belief and is entirely to be expected in this context. See Ibn Abil Hadīd, *Sharh-i Nahj al-Balāghah*, vol. 2, commentary on Sermon 30, pp. 126-161 and pp. 324-333; vol. 3, commentary on Sermon 43, 3-69; vol. 9, commentary on Sermon 135, pp. 3-30; and *Al-Ghadīr*, vol. 8, pp. 97-323. Worthy of note, however, is the statement here that Abū Bakr and 'Umar adhered to the example of the Prophet in their personal lives. See also the statement on p. 37. [Pub.]

[213] Hijāz: the region in Western Arabia that includes Mecca and Medina.

[54a] *Bihār al-Anwār*, vol. 40, p. 324.

If this mode of conduct had been preserved, and government had retained its Islamic form, there would have been no monarchy and no empire, no usurpation of the lives and property of the people, no oppression and plunder, no encroachment on the public treasury, no vice and abomination. Most forms of corruption originate with the ruling class, the tyrannical ruling family and the libertines that associate with them. It is these rulers who establish centers of vice and corruption, who build centers of vice and wine-drinking, and spend the income of the religious endowments constructing cinemas.[214]

If it were not for these profligate royal ceremonies,[215] this reckless spending, this constant embezzlement, there would never be any deficit in the national budget forcing us to bow in submission before America and Britain and request aid or a loan from them. Our country has become needy on account of this reckless spending, this endless embezzlement, for are we lacking in oil? Do we have no minerals, no natural resources? We have everything, but this parasitism, this embezzlement, this profligacy—all at the expense of the people and the public treasury—have reduced us to a wretched state. Otherwise he [the Shāh] would not need to go all the way to America and bow down before that ruffian's desk, begging for help.

In addition, superfluous bureaucracies and the system of file-keeping and paper-shuffling that is enforced in them, all of which are totally alien to Islam, impose further expenditures on our national budget not less in quantity than the illicit expenditures of the first category. This administrative system has nothing to do with Islam. These superfluous formalities, which cause our people nothing but expense, trouble, and delay, have no place in Islam. For example, the method established by Islam for enforcing people's rights, adjudicating disputes, and executing judgments is at once simple, practical, and swift. When the juridical methods of Islam were applied, the *sharī'ah* judge in each town, assisted only by two bailiffs and with only a pen and inkpot at his disposal, would swiftly resolve disputes among people and send them about their business. But now the bureaucratic organization of the Ministry of Justice has attained unimaginable proportions, and is, in addition, quite incapable of producing results.

It is things like these that make our country needy and produce nothing but expense and delay.

The qualifications essential for the ruler drive directly from the nature and form of Islamic government. In addition to general qualifications like intelligence and administrative ability, there are two other essential qualifications: knowledge of the law and justice.[216]

After the death of the Prophet (s), difference arose concerning the identity of the person who was to succeed him, but all the Muslims were in agreement that his successor should be someone knowledgeable and accomplished; there was disagreement only about his identity.

Since Islamic government is a government of law, knowledge of the law is necessary for the ruler, as has been laid down in tradition. Indeed such knowledge is necessary not only for the ruler, but also for anyone holding a post or exercising some

---

[214] After the Revolution, extensive evidence came to light of misappropriation of the religious endowment. Land was being given to cabaret singers and members of the royal family by the state-controlled administration of the endowments. See the articles on this subject in the Tehran daily *Kayhān*, Isfand 27, 1357/March 18, 1979. Concerning attempts by the regime to build a cinema in Qum, see S.H.R., *Barrasī va Tahlīlī az Nihzat-i Imām Khumaynī* (Najaf? 1356 Sh./1977), pp. 103-104.

[215] A reference to the coronation ceremonies of 1967.

[216] Concerning the precise meaning of "justice," see n. 21 above.

government function. The ruler, however, must surpass all others in knowledge. In laying claim to the Imamate, our Imāms also argued that the ruler must be more learned than everyone else.[57a] The objections raised by the Shī'i *'ulamā* are also to the same effect. A certain person asked the caliph a point of law and he was unable to answer; he was therefore unfit for the position of leader and successor to the Prophet (s). Or again, a certain act he performed was contrary to the laws of Islam; hence he was unworthy for his high post.[217]

Knowledge of the law and justice, then, constitute fundamental qualifications in the view of the Muslims. Other matters have no importance or relevance in this connection. Knowledge of the nature of the angels, for example, or of the attributes of the Creator, Exalted and Almighty, is of no relevance to the question of leadership. In the same vein, one who knows all the natural sciences, uncovers all the secrets of nature, or has a good knowledge of music, does not thereby qualify for leadership or acquire any priority in the matter of exercising government over those who know the laws of Islam and are just. The sole matters relevant to rule, those that were mentioned and discussed in the time of the Most Noble Messenger (s), and our Imāms ('a), and were, in addition, unanimously accepted by the Muslims, are: (1) the knowledgeability of the ruler or caliph, i.e., his knowledge of the provisions and ordinances of Islam; and (2) his justice, i.e., his excellence in belief and morals.

Reason also dictates the necessity for these qualities, because Islamic government is a government of law, not the arbitrary rule of an individual over the people or the domination of a group of individuals over the whole people. If the ruler is unacquainted with the contents of the law, he is not fit to rule; for if he follows the legal pronouncements of others his power to govern will be impaired, but if, on the other hand, he does not follow such guidance, he will be unable to rule correctly and implement the laws of Islam. It is an established principle that "the *faqīh* has authority over the ruler."[58a] If the ruler adheres to Islam, he must necessarily submit to the *faqīh*, asking him about the laws and ordinances of Islam in order to implement them. This being the case, the true rulers are the *fuqahā*[218] themselves, and rulership ought officially to be theirs, to apply to them, not to those who are obliged to follow the guidance of the *fuqahā* on account of their own ignorance of the law.

Of course, it is not necessary for all officials, provincial governors, and administrators to know all the laws of Islam and be *fuqahā*; it is enough that they should know the laws pertaining to their functions and duties. Such was the case in the time of the Prophet (s), and the Commander of the Faithful ('a). The highest authority must possess the two qualities mentioned—comprehensive knowledge and justice—but his assistants, officials and those sent to the provinces need know only the laws relevant to their own tasks; on other matters they must consult the ruler.

The ruler must also possess excellence in morals and belief; he must be just and untainted by major sins. Anyone who wishes to enact the penalties provided by Islam (i.e., to implement the penal code), to supervise the public treasury and the income and expenditures of the state, and to have God assign to him the power to

---

[57a] Imām 'Ali ('a) said: "O men! The most qualified among men for the caliphate is he who is most capable and knowledgeable of Allah's commands." *Nahj al-Balāghah*, Sermon 172. See *Al-Ihtijāj*, vol. 1, p. 229; *Bihār al-Anwār*, vol. 25, "Kitāb al-Imāmah," "Bāb Jamī' fī Sifāt al-Imām," p. 116. [Pub.]

[217] The reference here is to certain shortcomings Shī'ah traditionally perceived in the exercise of rule by Abū Bakr. See 'Allāmah Hilli, *Kashf al-Murād fī Sharh Tajrīd al-I'tiqād*, 'Destination' (*Maqsad*) 5, 'Issue' (*Mas'alah*) 6. [Pub.]

[58a] Imām Ja'far as-Sādiq ('a) said: "The king is sovereign over the people while the scholar is the authority over the king." *Bihār al-Anwār*, vol. 1, "Kitāb al-'Ilm," sec. 1, *hadīth* 92, p. 183. [Pub.]

[218] *Fuqahā*: the plural of *faqīh* (see n. 1 above).

administer the affairs of His creatures must not be a sinner. God says in the Qur'an: "my vow does not embrace the wrongdoer" (2:124);[219] therefore, He will not assign such functions to an oppressor or sinner.

If the ruler is not just in granting the Muslims their rights, he will not conduct himself equitably in levying taxes and spending them correctly and in implementing the penal code. It becomes possible then for his assistants, helpers, and confidants to impose their will on society, diverting the public treasury to personal and frivolous use.

Thus, the view of the Shī'ah concerning government and the nature of the persons who should assume rule was clear from the time following the death of the Prophet (s) down to the beginning of the Occultation.[220] It is specified that the ruler should be foremost in knowledge of the laws and ordinances of Islam, and just in their implementation.

Now that we are in the time of the Occultation of the Imām ('a), it is still necessary that the ordinances of Islam relating to government be preserved and maintained, and that anarchy be prevented. Therefore, the establishment of government is still a necessity.

Reason also dictates that we establish a government in order to be able to ward off aggression and to defend the honor of the Muslims in case of attack. The *sharī'ah*, for its part, instructs us to be constantly ready to defend ourselves against those who wish to attack us. Government, with its judicial and executive organs, is also necessary to prevent individuals from encroaching on each other's rights. None of these purposes can be fulfilled by themselves; it is necessary for a government to be established. Since the establishment of a government and the administration of society necessitate, in turn, a budget and taxation, the Sacred Legislator has specified the nature of the budget and the taxes that are to be levied, such as *kharāj, khums, zakāt,* and so forth.

Now that no particular individual has been appointed by God, Exalted and Almighty, to assume the function of government in the time of Occultation, what must be done? Are we to abandon Islam? Do we no longer need it? Was Islam valid for only two hundred years? Or is it that Islam has clarified our duties in other respects but not with respect to government?

Not to have an Islamic government means leaving our boundaries unguarded. Can we afford to sit nonchalantly on our hands while our enemies do whatever they want? Even if we do put our signatures to what they do as an endorsement, still are failing to make an effective response. Is that the way it should be? Or is it rather that government is necessary, and that the function of government that existed from the beginning of Islam down to the time of the Twelfth Imām ('a) is still enjoined upon us by God after the Occultation even though He has appointed no particular individuals to the function?

The two qualities of knowledge of the law and justice are present in countless *fuqahā* of the present age. If they come together, they could establish a government of universal justice in the world.

---

[219] The words of God's since they are Qur'anic, but in the context in which they appear, the speaker is Abraham. After asking God that prophethood be vested in his progeny, Abraham excludes any of his descendants who might be wrongdoers from exercising the prophetic function. For an elaborate commentary on this verse (Q 2:124), see Mīr Ahmad 'Ali, *Text, Translation and Commentary of the Holy Qur'an* (Elmhurst, NY: Tahrike Tarsile Qur'an, Inc., 1988), pp. 146-154,

[220] Occultation: see n. 27 above.

If a worthy individual possessing these two qualities arises and establishes a government, he will posses the same authority as the Most Noble Messenger ('a) in the administration of society, and it will be the duty of all people to obey him.

The idea that the governmental power of the Most Noble Messenger (s) were greater than those of the Commander of the Faithful ('a), or that those of the Commander of the Faithful ('a) were greater than those of the *faqīh*, is false and erroneous. Naturally, the virtues of the Most Noble Messenger (s) were greater than those of the rest of mankind, and after him, the Commander of the Faithful was the most virtuous person in the world. But superiority with respect to spiritual virtues does not confer increased governmental powers. God has conferred upon government in the present age the same powers and authority that were held by the Most Noble Messenger and the Imāms ('a), with respect to equipping and mobilizing armies, appointing governors and officials, and levying taxes and expending them for the welfare of the Muslims. Now, however, it is no longer a question of a particular person; government devolves instead upon one who possesses the qualities of knowledge and justice.

When we say that after the Occultation, the just *faqīh* has the same authority that the Most Noble Messenger and the Imāms ('a) had, do not imagine that the status of the *faqīh* is identical to that of the Imāms and the Prophet ('a). For here we are not speaking of status, but rather of function. By "authority" we mean government, the administration of the country, and the implementation of the sacred laws of the *sharī'ah*. These constitute a serious, difficult duty but do not earn anyone extraordinary status or raise him above the level of common humanity. In other words, authority here has the meaning of government, administration, and execution of law; contrary to what many people believe, it is not a privilege, but a grave responsibility. The governance of the *faqīh* is a rational and extrinsic[221] matter; it exists only as a type of appointment, like the appointment of a guardian for a minor. With respect to duty and position, there is indeed no difference between the guardian of a nation and the guardian of a minor. It is as if the Imām were to appoint someone to the guardianship of a minor, to the governorship of a province, or to some other post. In cases like these, it is not reasonable that there would be a difference between the Prophet and the Imāms ('a), on the one hand, and the just *faqīh*, on the other.

For example, one of the concerns that the *faqīh* must attend to is the application of the penal provisions of Islam. Can there be any distinction in this respect between the Most Noble Messenger (s), the Imāms, and the *faqīh*? Will the *faqīh* inflict fewer lashes because his rank is lower? Now, the penalty for the fornicator is one hundred lashes. If the Prophet (s) applies the penalty, is he to inflict one hundred fifty lashes, the Commander of the Faithful ('a) one hundred, and, the *faqīh* fifty? The ruler supervises the executive power and has the duty of implementing God's laws; it makes no difference if he is the Most Noble Messenger (s), the Commander of the Faithful ('a) or the representative or judge he appointed to Basrah or Kūfah, or a *faqīh* in the present age.

Another one of the concerns of the Most Noble Messenger (s) and the Commander of the Faithful ('a) was the levying of taxes—*khums, zakāt, jizyah* and *kharāj* on taxable lands.[62a] Now when the Prophet (s) levied *zakāt*, how much did he

---

[221] The "governance" (*vilāyat*) of the *faqīh* is extrinsic (*i'tibārī*) to his person; he exercises it only by virtue of the acquired attribute of just *faqīh*.

[62a] Taxable lands: those acquired by the Muslims under the Prophet (s) or the Islamic ruler. These lands belong to all Muslims and therefore non-sellable. The Islamic government leases them and their accrued income is called *kharāj*.

levy? One-tenth in one place and one-twentieth elsewhere? And how did the Commander of the Faithful ('a) proceed when he became the ruler? And what now, if one of us becomes the foremost *faqīh* of the age and is able to enforce his authority? In these matters, can there be any difference in the authority of the Most Noble Messenger (s), that of 'Ali ('a), and that of the *faqīh*? God Almighty appointed the Prophet (s) in authority over all the Muslims; as long as he was alive, his authority extended over even 'Ali ('a). Afterwards, the Imām ('a) had authority over all the Muslims, even his own successor as Imām ('a); his commands relating to government were valid for everyone, and he could appoint and dismiss judges and governors.

The authority that the Prophet and the Imām ('a) had in establishing a government, executing laws, and administering affairs, exists also for the *faqīh*. But the *fuqahā* do not have absolute authority in the sense of having authority over all other *fuqahā* of their own time, being able to appoint or dismiss them. There is no hierarchy ranking one *faqīh* higher than another or endowing one with more authority than another.

Now that this much has been demonstrated, it is necessary that the *fuqahā* proceed, collectively or individually, to establish a government in order to implement the laws of Islam and protect its territory. If this task falls within the capabilities of a single person, he has personally incumbent upon him the duty to fulfill it; otherwise, it is a duty that devolves upon the *fuqahā* as a whole. Even if it is impossible to fulfill the task, the authority vested in the *fuqahā* is not voided, because it has been vested in them by God. If they can, they must collect taxes, such as *zakāt*, *khums*, and *kharāj*, spend them for the welfare of the Muslims, and also enact the penalties of the law. The fact that we are presently unable to establish a complete and comprehensive form of government does not mean that we should sit idle. Instead, we should perform, to whatever extent we can, the tasks that are needed by the Muslims and that pertain to the functions an Islamic government must assume.

To prove that government and authority belong to the Imām ('a) is not to imply that the Imām ('a) has no spiritual status. The Imām ('a) does indeed possess certain spiritual dimensions that are unconnected with their function as a ruler. The spiritual status of the Imām ('a) is a universal divine viceregency that is sometimes mentioned by the Imāms ('a). It is a viceregency pertaining to the whole of creation, by virtue of which all the atoms in the universe humble themselves before the holder of authority. It is one of the essential beliefs of our Shī'i school that no one can attain the spiritual status of the Imāms, not even the cherubim or the prophets.[222] In fact, according to the traditions that have been handed down to us, the Most Noble Messenger and the Imāms ('a) existed before the creation of the world in the form of lights situated beneath the divine throne; they were superior to other men even in the

---

[222] The "governance" (*vilāyat*) of the Imāms is intrinsic to their persons, unlike that of the *fuqahā*; moreover, its scope is not limited to men but embraces the whole of creation. They therefore exercise "cosmic governance" (*vilāyat-i takvīnī*), in part through the performance of miracles. This form of *vilāyat* is common to the Imāms and to the foremost of the prophets, who exercised a governmental function while also propagating a divine message. The statement here that "no one can attain the spiritual status of the Imāms, not even the cherubim or the prophets" thus carries the strict sense that the Imāms are superior to those prophets whose mission lacked the dimension of governmental leadership. Concerning the different types of *vilāyat*, see Murtazā Mutahhari, *Valīhā va Vilāyat-hā* (Qum, 1355 Sh./1975), which was translated into English by Mustajab Ansāri under the title *Master and Mastership* (Karachi: Islamic Seminary Publication, 1980) and by Yahyā Cooper as *Wilāyat: The Station of the Master* (Tehran: World Organization for Islamic Services, 1982)

sperm from which they grow and in their physical composition.[223] Their exalted station is limited only by the divine will, as indicated by the saying of Jibrā'īl ('a) recorded in the traditions on the *mi'rāj*: "Were I to draw closer by as much as the breadth of a finger, surely I would burn."[224] The Prophet (s) himself said: "We have states with God that are beyond the reach of the cherubim and the prophets."[225] It is a part of our belief that the Imāms too enjoy similar states, before the question of government even arises. For example, Fātimah ('a) also possessed these states, even though she was not a ruler, a judge, or a governor.[226] These states are quite distinct from the function of government. So when we say that Fātimah ('a) was neither a judge nor a ruler, this does not mean that she was like you and me, or that she has no spiritual superiority over us. Similarly, if someone says, in accordance with the Qur'an, that "The Prophet (s) has higher claims on the believers than their own selves" (33:6), he has attributed to him something more exalted than his right to govern the believers. We will not examine these matters further here, for they belong to the area of another science.

To assume the function of government does not in itself carry any particular merit or status; rather, it is a means for fulfilling the duty of implementing the law and establishing the Islamic order of justice. The Commander of the Faithful ('a) said to Ibn 'Abbās[67a] concerning the nature of government and command: "How much is this shoe worth?" Ibn 'Abbās replied: "Nothing". The Commander of Faithful ('a) then said: "Command over you is worth still less in my eyes, except for this: by means of ruling and commanding you I may be able to establish the right"—i.e., the laws and institutions of Islam—"and destroy the wrong"[227]—i.e., all impermissible and oppressive laws and institutions.

Rule and command, then, are in themselves only a means, and if this means is not employed for the good and for attaining noble aims, it has no value in the eyes of the men of God. Thus the Commander of the Faithful ('a) says in his sermon in *Nahj al-Balāghah*: "Were it not for the obligation imposed on me, forcing me to take up this task of government, I would abandon it."[228] It is evident, then, that to assume the function of government is to acquire a means, and not a spiritual station, for if government were spiritual station, nobody would be able to either usurp it or abandon it. Government and the exercise of command acquire value only when they become

---

[223] Concerning these attributes of the Imāms, see Henri Corbin, *Histoire de la philosophie islamique* (Paris, 1964), pp. 74 ff; Sayyid Saeed Akhtar Rizvi, *Imamate: Vicegerency of the Prophet*, anno. Sayyid Muhammad Akhtar Rizvi (Tehran: WOFIS, 1986); Sayyid Mujtabā Mūsāwi Lāri, *Imamate and Leadership*, trans. Hamid Algar (Qum: Foundation for Cultural Propagation in the World); Sayyid Muhammad Rizvi, *Shī'ism Imamate and Wilāyat* (Qum: Ansariyan Publications, 2000). [Pub.]

[224] The archangel Jibrā'īl (Gabriel) accompanied the Most Noble Messenger on his *mi'rāj* (ascension to the divine presence), but being of lowlier station than the Messenger, he was unable to endure the splendor of the divine presence. See *Bihār al-Anwār*, vol. 18, "*bāb ithbāt al-mi'rāj wa ma'nāhu wa kayfiyyatah*," p. 382. [Pub.]

[225] A well-known tradition relating to the *mi'rāj*.

[226] Fātimah, the daughter of the Prophet, shared in the exalted states of the Prophet and the Twelve Imāms in that she possessed the same quality of *'ismat* (divinely bestowed freedom from error and sin) that they did. As daughter of the Prophet and wife of the first Imām, she served, moreover, as a link between the Prophet and his successors. See Ibrāhīm Amīni and Sayyid Kāzim Qazvīni, *Fatima the Gracious*, trans. Abū Muhammad Ordoni (Qum: Ansariyan Publications) [Pub.]

[67a] Ibn 'Abbās: more fully, 'Abdullāh ibn 'Abbās ibn 'Abdul Muttalib (3 B.H.-68 A.H.) was a cousin of the Prophet and 'Ali, who learned the science of Qur'anic exegesis from the latter and known as "chief of the exegetes" and "scholar of the community". He had been one of Imām 'Ali's commanders in the Battles of Jamal, Siffīn and Nahrawan. [Pub.]

[227] *Nahj al-Balāghah*, Sermon 33, p. 76. [Pub.]

[228] *Nahj al-Balāghah*, p. 50.

the means for implementing the law of Islam and establishing the just Islamic order; then the person in charge of government may also earn some additional virtue and merit.

Some people, whose eyes have been dazzled by the things of this world, imagine that leadership and government represented in themselves dignity and high station for the Imāms, so that if others come to exercise power, the world will collapse. Now the Soviet ruler, the British Prime Minister, and the American President all exercise power, and they are all unbelievers. They are unbelievers, but they have political power and influence, which they use to execute anti-human laws and policies for the sake of their own interests.

It is the duty of the Imāms and the just *fuqahā* to use government institutions to execute divine law, to establish the just Islamic system, and serve mankind. Government in itself represents nothing but pain and trouble for them, but what are they to do? They have been given a duty, a mission to fulfill; the governance of the *faqīh* is nothing but the performance of a duty.

When explaining why he assumed the tasks of government and rule, the Commander of the Faithful ('a) declared that he did so for the sake of certain exalted aims, namely the establishment of justice and the abolition of injustice. He said, in effect: "O God, You know that it is not our purpose to acquire position and power, but rather to deliver the oppressed from the hands of the unjust. What impelled me to accept the task of command and rule over the people was this: God, Almighty and Exalted, has exacted a pledge from the scholars of religion and assigned the duty of not remaining silent in the face of the gluttony and self-indulgence of the unjust and the oppressor on the one hand, and the wasting hunger of the oppressed, on the other."[69a] He also said: "O God! You know well that the struggle we have waged has not been for the sake of winning political power, nor for seeking worldly goods and overflowing wealth." He went directly on to explain the goal for the sake of which he and his companions had been struggling and exerting themselves: "Rather it was our aim to restore and implement the luminous principles of Your religion and to reform the conduct of affairs in Your land, so that Your downtrodden servants might gain security and Your laws, which have remained unfulfilled and in abeyance, might be established and executed."[229]

The ruler who, by means of the organs of government and the power of command that are at his disposal, desires to attain the exalted aims of Islam, the same aims set forth by the Commander of the Faithful ('a), must possess the essential qualities to which we have already referred; that is, he must know the law and be just. The Commander of the Faithful ('a) mentions next the qualities essential in a ruler immediately after he has specified the aims of government: "O God! I was the first person that turned toward You by accepting Your religion as soon as I heard your Messenger (s) declare it. No one preceded me in prayer except the Messenger (s) himself. And you, O people! You know well that it is not fitting that one who is greedy and parsimonious should attain rule and authority over the honor, lives, and income of the Muslims, and the laws and ordinances enforced among them, and also leadership of them.

"Furthermore, he should not be ignorant and unaware of the law, lest in his ignorance he mislead the people. He must not be unjust and harsh, causing the people to cease all traffic and dealing with him because of his oppressiveness. Nor must he

---

[69a] *Nahj al-Balāghah*, Sermon 3 (*Shaqshaqiyyah Sermon*). [Pub.]
[229] *Nahj al-Balāghah*, pp. 188-189.

37

fear states, so that he seeks the friendship of some and treats others with enmity. He must refrain from accepting bribes when he sits in judgment, so that the rights of men are trampled underfoot and the claimant does not receive his due. He must not leave the practice of the Prophet (s) and law in abeyance, so that the community falls into misguidance and peril."[230]

Notice how this discourse revolves around two points, knowledge and justice, and how the Commander of the Faithful ('a) regards them as necessary qualities of the ruler. In the expression: "He should not be ignorant and unaware of the law, lest in his ignorance he mislead the people," the emphasis is upon knowledge, while in the remaining sentences the emphasis is upon justice, in its true sense. The true sense of justice is that the ruler should conduct himself like the Commander of the Faithful ('a) in his dealings with other states, in his relations and transactions with the people, in passing sentence and giving judgment, and in distributing the public income. To put it differently, the ruler should adhere to the program of rule that the Commander of the Faithful ('a) assigned to Mālik Ashtar[231]—in reality, to all rulers and governors, for it is something like a circular addressed to all who exercise rule. If the *fuqahā* become rulers, they too should consider it as their set of instructions.

Here is a narration totally without ambiguity. The Commander of the Faithful ('a) relates that the Most Noble Messenger (s) said: "O God! Have mercy on those that succeed me." He repeated this thrice and was then asked: "O Messenger of God, who are those that succeed you?" He replied: "They are those that come after me, transmit my traditions and practice, and teach them to the people after me."

Shaykh Sadūq[232] (may God's mercy be upon him) has related this narration with five chains of transmission (actually four, since two of them are similar in certain respects) in the following books: *Jāmiʿ al-Akhbār*, *ʿUyūn Akhbār ar-Ridhā*, and *Al-Majālis*.[233]

Among the cases where this tradition has been designated as *musnad*,[234] in one instance we find the words "and teach them," and in other instances we find, "and teach them to the people." Whenever the tradition is designated as *mursal*,[235] we find only the beginning of the sentence, with the phrase "and teach them to the people after me" completely omitted.

We can make either of two assumptions with respect to this tradition. First, it is the only instance of the tradition, and the phrase beginning "and teach them" either

---

[230] *Nahj al-Balāghah*, Sermon 131 on p. 31 of the present volume. [Pub.]

[231] Mālik Ashtar: more fully, Mālik ibn Hārith from Nakha'a and famous as al-Ashtar, was among the prominent commanders of Imām ʿAlī's army and the governor appointed to Egypt by Imām ʿAlī. He accompanied the Imām in the Battles of Jamal and Siffīn. On his way to Egypt, he was killed through the conspiracy of Muʿāwiyah. For the text of the Imām's famous instructions to him before setting forth to Egypt, see *Nahj al-Balāghah*, Letter 53, pp. 426-445. A complete translation is contained in William C. Chittick, *A Shīʿite Anthology* (Albany, N.Y., 1980), pp. 68-82. [Pub.]

[232] Shaykh Sadūq: also known as Ibn Babūyah, one of the most important of the early Shīʿi scholars. He died in 381/991. For his short biography and works, see the introduction of Shaykh as-Sadūq, *Iʿtiqādātu 'l-Imāmiyyah: A Shīʿite Creed*, 3rd Ed., trans. Asaf A. A. Fyzee (Tehran: World Organization for Islamic Services, 1999), pp. 6-23. [Pub.]

[233] *Jāmiʿ al-Akhbār*: a collection of Shīʿī traditions. *ʿUyūn Akhbār ar-Ridhā*: a collection of traditions relating to Imām Ridā, compiled by Shaykh Sadūq for Sāhib ibn ʿAbbād, celebrated minister of the Buwayhid dynasty and patron of learning. *Al-Majālis*: also known as *al-Amali*, the record of a series of discourses given by Shaykh Sadūq concerning all aspects of Shīʿi Islam.

[234] *Musnad*: a *hadīth* that goes back to the Prophet by an unbroken chain of transmission.

[235] *Mursal*: a *hadīth* whose chain of transmission goes only as far back as a "follower" (member of the second generation of Islam) who does not mention the name of the companion of the Prophet from whom he heard it.

was later added to the end, or was indeed a part of the tradition but was later omitted in certain versions. The second alternative is more probable. For if the phrase were added, we could not say that it was as the result of mistake or error, given that the tradition was handed down by several chain of transmission and the respective narrators lived at great distances from each other—one in Balkh, another in Nishābūr, and still another elsewhere. Nor is it possible that this phrase was deliberately added; it is highly unlikely that it would have occurred to each of several people living far apart from each other to add such a sentence to the tradition. Therefore, if it is a single narration, we can assert with certainly that either the phrase beginning, "and teach them" was omitted from one of the versions recorded by Shaykh Sadūq (or overlooked by the copyists who wrote down his work), or Shaykh Sadūq himself failed to mention it for some other reason.

The second assumption would be that there are two separate traditions; one without the phrase "and teach them..." and the other with it. If the phrase is part of the tradition, it certainly does not apply to those whose task is simply the narration of tradition and who are not competent to express an independent juridical opinion or judgment. There are certain scholars of tradition who do not understand *hadīth* at all; as implied in the saying: "Many a scholar of law falls short of being a *faqīh*," they are merely a vehicle for the recording, collecting and writing down of traditions and narrations and for placing them at the disposal of the people. It cannot be said of such scholars that they are the successors of the Prophet, teaching the sciences of Islam.[236] Their efforts on behalf of Islam and the Muslims are of course most valuable, and many scholars of tradition have indeed also been *fuqahā*, competent to express an independent opinion; e.g., Kulayni,[237] Shaykh Sadūq,[238] and his father (God's mercy on all of them). These three were *fuqahā*, and they taught the ordinances and sciences of Islam to the people. When we say that Shaykh Sadūq differed from Shaykh Mufīd,[239] we do not mean that Shaykh Sadūq was unlearned in *fiqh*,[240] or that he was less learned than Shaykh Mufīd. Shaykh Sadūq was, after all, the person who elucidated all the principles and secondaries of religion in a single sitting. He differed from Shaykh Mufīd and others like him in that they were *mujtahids* who brought their own reasoning to bear on traditions and narrations, while Shaykh Sadūq was a *faqīh* who did not have recourse to his own reasoning, or did so only rarely.

The phrase we are discussing applies to those who expound the sciences of Islam, who expound the ordinances of Islam, and who educate the people in Islam, preparing them to instruct others in turn. In the same way, the Most Noble Messenger (s), and the Imāms (`a) proclaimed and expounded the ordinances of Islam; they had teaching circles where they gave the benefit of their learning to several thousand

---

[236] That is, there is a functional distinction between the scholar of *hadīth* and the *faqīh*, although it is possible for a single individual to embody the two functions.

[237] Kulayni: see n. 30 above.

[238] Shaykh Sadūq: see n. 73 above.

[239] Shaykh Mufīd: the common designation of Abū 'Abdullāh Muhammad ibn Muhammad ibn Nu'mān al-Hārithi (d. 413/1022) who was a great Shī'ah jurist, traditionist and scholar of scholasticism. Notable among his disciples were Sayyid Murtadā 'Allama al-Hudā, Sayyid Rāzi, Shaykh Tūsi, and Najashi. Aroung 200 works are attributed to him, from which we can cite *Kitāb al-Irshad*, *Ikhtisās*, *Awā'il al-Maqālāt*, *'Amali*, and *Maqna'ah*. See Shaykh Mufīd, *Kitāb al-Irshād: The Book of Guidance into the Lives of the Twelve Imāms*, trans. I.K.A. Howard (Karachi: Islamic Seminary Publications), introduction, pp. xxi-xxvii; Martin J. McDermott, *The Theology of al-Shaikh al-Mufīd* (Beirut: Dar al-Mashreq, 1978), introduction, pp. 8-45. [Pub.]

[240] *Fiqh*: jurisprudence; the discipline devoted to the study of the principles and ordinances of Islamic law.

people, whose duty it was, in turn, to teach others. That is the meaning implied in the phrase "and teach the people...": disseminating the knowledge of Islam among the people and conveying to them the ordinances of Islam. If we believe that Islam is for all the people in the world, it becomes obvious to every rational mind that the Muslims, and particularly the scholars among them, have the duty of disseminating knowledge of Islam and its ordinances and acquainting the people of the world with them.

If we suppose that the phrase "and teach them to the people" does not belong to the end of the *hadīth*, then we must see what the Prophet (s) might have meant in his saying: "O God! Have mercy on those that succeed me: those that come after me and transmit my traditions and practice." The tradition, even in this form, still would not apply to those who merely relate traditions without being *fuqahā*. For the divine practices and norms constituting the totality of the ordinances of Islam are known as the practice of the Prophet (s) by virtue of the fact that they were revealed to him. So anyone who wishes to disseminate the practices of the Most Noble Messenger (s) must know all the ordinances of God; he must be able to distinguish the authentic from the false, those of absolute from those of limited application, and the general from the specific. Further, he must be able to discern rational categories, distinguish between traditions originating in circumstances of *taqiyyah*[241] and those originating otherwise, and be fully conversant with all the necessary criteria that have been specified. Traditionists who have not attained the level of *ijtihād*[242] and who merely transmit *hadith* know nothing about all this; hence, they are incapable of discerning the true practice of the Messenger of God (s). Mere transmission could have no value in the eyes of the Messenger, and it was certainly not his desire that phrases like: "The Messenger of God said," or "It is related on the authority of the Messenger of God" should gain currency among the people, if the sentences prefaced by these phrases were counterfeited and not his. What he desired instead was that his true practice should be disseminated among the people and the real ordinances of Islam spread among them. The tradition: "Whoever preserves for my people forty traditions will be resurrected by God as a *faqīh*"[243] and similar traditions praising the dissemination of *hadith* do not pertain to traditionists who have no concept of the nature of tradition. They pertain to those who are able to distinguish the true narration of the Most Noble Messenger (s) in accordance with the true ordinances of Islam. Such persons are none other than the *mujtahids* and the *fuqahā*; they are the ones able to assess all different aspects and implications of a ruling, and to deduce the true ordinances of Islam on the basis of the criteria they have inherited from the Imāms ('a). They are the successors of the Most Noble Messenger (s), disseminating the divine ordinances and instructing men in the sciences of Islam. It is for them that the Prophet (s) prayed when he said, "O God! Have mercy on my successors."

There is no doubt, therefore, that the tradition: "O God! Have mercy on my successors" does not relate to the transmitters of tradition who are mere scribes; a scribe cannot be a successor to the Prophet (s). The successors are the *fuqahā* of Islam. Dissemination of the ordinances of Islam, as well as the teaching and instruction of the people, is the duty of *fuqahā* who are just. For if they are not just, they will be like those who forged traditions harmful to Islam, like Samūrah ibn

---

[241] *Taqiyyah*: see n. 16 above.

[242] *Ijtihād*: see n. 4 above.

[243] A well-known tradition that has led to the compilation of anthologies of forty *hadīth* intended for memorization by those who wish to attain the promised reward.

Jundab,[244] who forged traditions hostile to the Commander of the Faithful ('a). And if they are not *fuqahā*, they cannot comprehend the nature of *fiqh* and the ordinances of Islam, and they may disseminate thousands of traditions in praise of kings that have been forged by the agents of the oppressors and pseudo-scholars attached to royal courts. It is easy to see what results they obtained on the basis of the two weak traditions that they set up against the Qur'an, with its insistent commands to rise up against kings and its injunctions to Moses to rebel against the Pharaoh.[245] Quite apart from the Glorious Qur'an, there are numerous traditions exhorting men to struggle against tyrants and those who pervert religion.[246] Lazy people among us have laid these aside and, relying on these two weak *hadīths* that may well have been forged by court preachers, tell us we must make peace with kings and give our allegiance to the court. If they were truly acquainted with tradition and knowledgeable about religion, they would act instead in accordance with the numerous traditions that denounce the oppressors. If it happens that they are acquainted with tradition, then we must conclude that, they do not have the quality of justice. For, not being just and failing to eschew sin, they overlook the Qur'an and all the narration that condemn the oppressor, and concentrate instead on those two weak *hadith*. It is the appetites of their stomachs that cause them to cling to them, not knowledge. Appetite and ambition make men subservient to royal courts; true tradition does not.

In any event, the dissemination of the sciences of Islam and the proclamation of its ordinances are the task of the just *fuqahā*—those who are able to distinguish the true ordinances from the false, and the traditions of the Imāms ('a) arising in conditions of *taqiyyah* from those originating otherwise. For we know that our Imāms were sometimes subjected to conditions that prevented them from pronouncing a true ordinance; they were exposed to tyrannical and oppressive rulers who imposed *taqiyyah* and fear upon them. Naturally, their fear was for religion not themselves, and if they had not observed *taqiyyah* in certain circumstances, oppressive rulers would have entirely rooted out true religion.

There cannot be the least doubt that the tradition we have been discussing refers to the governance of the *faqih*, for to be a successor means to succeed to all the functions of prophethood. In this respect what is implied by the sentence: "O God! Have mercy on my successors" is no less than what is implied by the sentence: " 'Ali is my successor," since the meaning of successorship is the same in both cases. The phrase "who come after me and transmit my traditions" serves to designate the successors, not to define succession, for succession was a well-known concept in the first age of Islam and did not require elucidation. Moreover, the person who asked the Prophet (s), whom he meant by his successors was not enquiring after the meaning of successorship; he was requesting the Prophet (s) to specify those whom he meant, as he indeed did in his reply. It is remarkable that nobody has taken the phrase: " 'Ali is

---

[244] Samūrah ibn Jundab: more fully, Abū Sa'īd Samūrah ibn Jundab al-Qazāri, a companion of the Prophet who accompanied him in numerous battles. He later settled in Basrah, where he temporarily acted as governor on a number of occasions during the rule of Mu'āwiyah, first Umayyad caliph.

[245] One of the two weak traditions referred to here is probably: "The sultan is the shadow of God upon earth; whoever respects him, respects God, and whoever affronts him, affronts God." For a critique of this alleged tradition, see Nāsir ad-Dīn al-Albāni, *Silsilat al-Āhādīth ad-Da'īfa wa'l-Maudū'a* (Damascus, 1384/ 1964), I, i, 98. The other weak tradition may be that says: 'Whoever wishes long life for a king will be resurrected together with him'. See *Islam and Revolution*, p. 220.

[246] For example, there is a tradition that says: "A word of truth spoken in the presence of an unjust ruler is a meritorious form of *jihād*," and two others close with the phrase "there is no obeying the one who disobeys God." For these and similar traditions, see 'Abdullāh Fahd an-Nafīsi, *'Indamā yahkum al-Islām* (London, n.d.), pp. 142-146.

my successor," or "the Imāms are my successors," as referring to the simple task of issuing juridical opinions; instead they derive the tasks of successorship and government from them, whereas they hesitated to draw the same conclusion from the words "my successors" in the tradition under consideration. This is solely because they have imagined that succession to the position of the Most Noble Messenger (s) has been limited or restricted to certain people, and that since each of the Imāms was a successor, the religious scholars cannot act as successors, rulers, and governors. The result is that Islam must be without any leader to care for it, the ordinances of Islam must be in abeyance, the frontiers of Islam must be at the mercy of the enemies of religion, and various kinds of perversion that have nothing to do with Islam are gaining currency.

Muhammad ibn Yaḥyā relates, on the authority of Ahmad ibn Muhammad, who heard it from Ibn Mahbūb, who was informed of it by 'Ali ibn Abi Hamzah, that the Imām Abu 'l-Hasan, son of Ja'far,[247] ('a) said: "whenever a believer dies, the angels weep, together with the ground where he engaged in the worship of God and the gates of heaven that he would enter by means of his good deeds. A crack will appear in the fortress of Islam, that naught can repair, for believers who are *fuqahā* are the fortresses of Islam, like the encircling walls that protect a city."[248]

In the same chapter of *Al-Kāfi*, is another version of this tradition, which reads: "Whenever a believer who is a *faqih*..." instead of "Whenever a believer..." In contrast, at the beginning of the version we have cited, the expression "who is a *faqih*" is missing. Later in the second version, however, when the cause for the angels' weeping is adduced, the expression "believers who are *fuqahā*" does occur. This makes it clear that the word *faqih* was omitted at the beginning of the tradition, particularly since the concepts "fortress of Islam" and "encircling walls" and the like are fully appropriate to the *faqih*.

The saying of the Imām ('a) that "believers who are *fuqaha* are the fortresses of Islam" actually ascribes to the *fuqahā* the duty of being guardians of the beliefs, ordinances, and institutions of Islam. It is clear that these words of the Imām ('a) are not an expression of ceremonial courtesy, like the words we sometimes exchange with each other (I call you "Support of the Sharī'ah," and you bestow the same title on me in return!). Nor do they have any similarity to the titles we use in addressing a letter to someone: "His Noble Excellency, the Proof of Islam."

If a *faqīh* sits in the corner of his dwelling and does not intervene in any of the affairs of society, neither preserving the laws of Islam and disseminating its ordinances, nor in any way participating in the affairs of the Muslims or having any care for them, can he be called "the fortress of Islam" or the protector of Islam?

If the leader of a government tells an official or a commander, "Go and guard such-and-such an area," will the duty of guarding that he has assumed permit him to go home and sleep, allowing the enemy to come and ravage that area? Or should he, on the contrary, strive to protect that area in whatever way he can?

Now if you say that we are preserving at least some of the ordinances of Islam, let me ask you this question. Are you implementing the penal law of Islam and the sanctions it provides? You will have to answer no.

So a crack has appeared in the protective wall surrounding Islam, despite your supposedly being its guardians.

---

[247] Imām Abū 'l-Hasan Mūsā, son of Ja'far: seventh of the Twelve Imāms, and generally known as Imām Mūsā al-Kāzim. He was born in Medina in 128/744 and died in prison in Baghdad in 183/799.
[248] See Shaykh Abū Ja'far al-Kulayni, *al-Kāfi*, Eng. trans. Sayyid Muhammad Hasan Rizvi (Tehran: WOFIS, 1398/1978), I, ii, 94-95.

Then I ask you: Are you guarding the frontiers of Islam and the territorial integrity of the Islamic homeland? To this, your answer may be: "No, our task is only to pray!"

This means that a piece of the wall has collapsed.

Now I ask you: Are you taking from the rich what they owe the poor and passing it on to them? For that is your Islamic duty, to take from the rich and give to the poor. Your answer may be, in effect: "No, this is none of our concern! God willing, others will come and perform this task."

Then another part of the wall will have collapsed, and your situation will be like that of Shāh Sultān Husayn waiting for the fall of Isfahan.[249]

What kind of fortress is this? Each of the corners is occupied by some "pillar of Islam," but all he can do is offer excuses when put to the test. Is that what we mean by "fortress"?

The meaning of the statement of the Imām ('a) that the *fuqahā* are the fortresses of Islam is that they have a duty to protect Islam and that they must do whatever is necessary to fulfill that duty. It is one of the most important duties and, moreover, an absolute duty, not a conditional one. It is an issue to which the *fuqahā* of Islam must pay particular attention. The religious teaching institution must give due thought to the matter and equip itself with the means and strength necessary to protect Islam in the fullest possible sense, just as the Most Noble Messenger (s) and the Imāms ('a) were the guardians of Islam, protecting its beliefs, ordinances and institutions in the most comprehensive manner.

We have abandoned almost all aspects of our duty, restricting ourselves to passing on, from one generation to the next, certain parts of Islamic law and discussing them among ourselves. Many of the ordinances of Islam have virtually become part of the occult sciences, and Islam itself has become a stranger;[250] only its name has survived.

All the penal provisions of Islam, which represent the best penal code ever devised for humanity, have been completely forgotten; nothing but their name has survived. As for the Qur'anic verses stipulating penalties and sanctions, "Nothing remains of them but their recitation."[251] For example, we recite the verse: "Administer to the adulterer and the adulteress a hundred lashes each"(24:2), but we do not know what to do when confronted with a case of adultery. We merely recite the verse in order to improve the quality of our recitation and to give each sound its full value. The actual situation prevailing in our society, the present state of the Islamic community, the prevalence of lewdness and corruption, the protection and support extended by our governments to adultery—none of this concern us! It is enough that we understand what penalties have been provided for the adulterer and adulteress without attempting to secure their implementation or otherwise struggling against the existence of adultery in our society!

I ask you, is that the way the Most Noble Messenger (s) conduct himself? Did he content himself with reciting the Qur'an, then lay it aside and neglect to ensure the

---

[249] Shāh Sultān Husayn was the last monarch of the Safavid dynasty, which ruled over Iran from the beginning of the sixteenth century until the second decade of the eighteenth. Among the least competent of the Safavid rulers, he devoted his energies to debauchery and failed to organize the defense of his capital city, Isfahan, against Afghan invaders, to whom it fell in 1722 after a six-month siege. See L. Lockhart, *The Fall of the Safavid Dynasty* (Cambridge, 1958), pp. 144-170.

[250] See n. 2 above.

[251] Part of a long *hadīth* concerning a dream in which the Messenger foresaw the misdeeds of the Umayyads.

implementation of its penal provisions? Was it the practice of the successors of the Prophet (s) to entrust matters to the people and tell them, "I have no further concern with you"? Or, on the contrary, did they decree penalties for various classes of offender—whippings, stonings, perpetual imprisonment, banishment? Examine the sections of Islamic law relating to penal law and blood money: you will see that all of these matters are part of Islam and part of the reason for the coming of Islam. Islam came in order to establish order in society; leadership[252] and government are for the sake of ordering the affairs of society.

It is our duty to preserve Islam. This duty is one of the most important obligations incumbent upon us; it is more necessary even than prayer and fasting. It is for the sake of fulfilling this duty that blood must sometimes be shed. There is no blood more precious than that of Imām Husayn ('a), yet it was shed for the sake of Islam, because of the precious nature of Islam. We must understand this matter well and convey it to others. You can be the true successors to the Prophet (s) as the guardians of Islam only if you teach Islam to the people; do not say, "We will wait until the coming of the Imām of the Age ('a)." Would you consider postponing your prayer until the coming of the Imām? The preservation of Islam is even more important than prayer. Do not follow the logic of the governor of Khumayn[253] who used to say, "We must promote sin so that the Imām of the Age ('a) will come. If sin does not prevail, he will not manifest himself!"[254] Do not sit here simply debating among yourselves. Study all the ordinances of Islam and propagate all aspects of the truth by writing and publishing pamphlets. It cannot fail to have an effect, as my own experience testifies.

'Ali relates, on the authority of his father, from an-Nawfali, who had it from as-Sukūni, who was told it by Abu 'Abdullāh ('a), that the Most Noble Messenger (s) said, "The *fuqahā* are the trustees of the prophets ('a), as long as they do not concern themselves with the illicit desires, pleasures, and wealth of the world." The Prophet (s) was then asked: "O Messenger of God! How may we know if they do so concern themselves?" He replied: "By seeing whether they follow the ruling power. If they do that, fear for your religion and shun them."[255] Examination of the whole of this *hadith* would involve us in a lengthy discussion. We will speak only about the phrase: "The *fuqahā* are the trustees of the prophets ('a)," since it is what interests us here because of its relevance to the topic of the governance of *faqīh*.

First, we must see what duties, powers, and functions the prophets ('a) had in order to discover what the duties of the *fuqahā*, the trustees and successors of the prophets ('a), are in turn.

In accordance with both wisdom and the essential nature of religion, the purpose in sending the prophets ('a) and the task of the prophets ('a) cannot be simply the delivery of judgments concerning a particular problem or the expounding of the ordinances of religion. These judgments and ordinances were not revealed to the Prophet (s) in order for him and the Imāms ('a) to convey them truthfully to the people as series of divinely appointed *muftis*,[256] and then to pass this trust on in turn to the *fuqahā*, so that they might likewise convey them to the people without any

---

[252] The expression translated here as "leadership" is *imāmat-i i'tibāri*; see n. 62 above.

[253] Khumayn: the native town of Imām Khomeini.

[254] Since the Imām of the Age—i.e., the Twelfth Imām—will emerge from his occultation at the time when injustice fills the earth, it has sometimes been thought that all positive action to remedy injustice must be postponed until his coming.

[255] See Kulayni, *al-Kāfi*, I, ii, 188-119.

[256] *Mufti*: a scholar who pronounces an authoritative opinion (*fatwā*) on a point of law.

44

distortion. The meaning of the expression: "The *fuqahā* are the trustees of the prophets ('a)" is not that the *fuqahā* are the trustees simply with respect to the giving of juridical opinions. For in fact the most important function of the prophets ('a) is the establishment of a just social system through the implementation of laws and ordinances (which is naturally accompanied by the exposition and dissemination of the divine teachings and beliefs). This emerges clearly from the following Qur'anic verse: "Verily We have sent Our messengers with clear signs, and sent down with them the Book and the Balance, in order that men might live in equity" (57:25). The general purpose for the sending of prophets ('a), then, is so that men's lives may be ordered and arranged on the basis of just social relations and true humanity may be established among men. This is possible only by establishing government and implementing laws, whether this is accomplished by the prophet himself, as was the case with the Most Noble Messenger (s), or by the followers who come after him.

God Almighty says concerning the *khums*: "Know that of whatever booty you capture, a fifth belongs to God and His Messenger and to your kinsmen"(8:41). Concerning *zakāt* He says: "Levy a tax on their property"(9:103). There are also other divine commands concerning other forms of taxation. Now the Most Noble Messenger (s) had the duty not only of expounding these ordinances, but also of implementing them; just as he was to proclaim them to the people, he was also to put them into practice. He was to levy taxes, such as *khums, zakāt* and *kharāj*, and spend the resulting income for the benefit of the Muslims; establish justice among peoples and among the members of the community; implement the laws and protect the frontiers and independence of the country; and prevent anyone from misusing or embezzling the finances of the Islamic state.

Now God Almighty appointed the Most Noble Messenger (s) head of the community and made it a duty for men to obey him: "Obey God and obey the Messenger and the holders of authority from among you" (4:59). The purpose for this was not so that we would accept and conform to whatever judgment the Prophet (s) delivered. Conformity to the ordinances of religion is obedience to God; all activities that are conducted in accordance with divine ordinances, whether or not they are ritual functions, are a form of obedience to God. Following the Most Noble Messenger (s), then, is not conforming to divine ordinances; it is something else. Of course, obeying the Most Noble Messenger (s) is, in a certain sense, obeying God; we obey the Prophet (s) because God has commanded us to do so. But if, for example, the Prophet (s), in his capacity as leader and guide of Islamic society, orders everybody to join the army of Usāmah,[257] so that no one has the right to hold back, it is the command of the Prophet (s), not the command of God. God has entrusted to him the task of government and command, and accordingly, in conformity with the interests of the Muslims, he arranges for the equipping and mobilization of the army, and appoints or dismisses governors and judges.

This being the case, the principle: "The *fuqahā* are the trustees of the prophets ('a)" means that all of the tasks entrusted to the prophets ('a) must also be fulfilled by the just *fuqahā* as a matter of duty. Justice, it is true; is a more comprehensive concept than trustworthiness and it is possible that someone may be trustworthy with respect to financial affairs, but not just in a more general sense.[258] However, those designated in the principle: "The *fuqahā* are the trustees of the prophets ('a)" are those who do not fail to observe any ordinances of the law, and who are pure and unsullied, as is

---

[257] Usāmah: that is, Usāmah ibn Zayd, a beloved companion of the Prophet who was placed in charge of a military expedition when he was only eighteen. He died in 59/679.
[258] See n. 21 above.

45

implied by the conditional statement: "as long as they do not concern themselves with the illicit desires, pleasures, and wealth of this world"---that is, as long as they do not sink into the morass of worldly ambition. If a *faqīh* has as his aim the accumulation of worldly wealth, he is longer just and cannot be the trustee of the Most Noble Messenger ('a) and the executor of the ordinances of Islam. It is only the just *fuqahā* who may correctly implement the ordinances of Islam and firmly establish its institutions, executing the penal provisions of Islamic law and preserving the boundaries and territorial integrity of the Islamic homeland. In short, implementation of all laws relating to government devolves upon the *fuqahā*: the collection of *khums*, *zakāt*, *sadaqah*, *jizyah*, and *kharāj* and the expenditure of the money thus collected in accordance with the public interest; the implementation of the penal provisions of the law and the enactment of retribution (which must take place under the direct supervision of the ruler, failing which the next-of-kin of the murdered person has no authority to act); the guarding of the frontiers; and the securing of public order.

Just as the Most Noble Messenger (s) was entrusted with the implementation of divine ordinances and the establishment of the institutions of Islam, and just as God Almighty set him up over the Muslims as their leader and ruler, making obedience to him obligatory, so, too, the just *fuqahā* must be leaders and rulers, implementing divine ordinances and establishing the institutions of Islam.

Since Islamic government is a government of law, those acquainted with the law, or more precisely, with religion—i.e., the *fuqahā*—must supervise its functioning. It is they who supervise all executive and administrative affairs of the country, together with all planning.

The *fuqahā* are the trustees who implement the divine ordinances in levying taxes, guarding the frontiers, and executing the penal provisions of the law. They must not allow the laws of Islam to remain in abeyance, or their operation to be effected by either defect or excess. If a *faqīh* wishes to punish an adulterer, he must give him one hundred lashes in the presence of the people, in the exact manner that has been specified. He does not have the right to inflict one additional lash, to curse the offender, to slap him, or to imprison him for a single day. Similarly, when it comes to the levying of taxes, he must act in accordance with the criteria and the laws of Islam; he does not have the right to tax even a *shāhi*[259] in excess of what the law provides. He must not let disorder enter the affairs of the public treasury or even so much as a *shāhi* be lost. If a *faqīh* acts in contradiction to the criteria of Islam (God forbid!), then he will automatically be dismissed from his post, since he will have forfeited his quality of trustee.

Law is actually the ruler; the security for all is guaranteed by law, and law is their refuge. Muslims and the people in general are free within the limits laid down by the law; when they are acting in accordance with the provisions of the law, no one has the right to tell them, "Sit here," or "Go there." An Islamic government does not resemble states where the people are deprived of all security and everyone sits at home trembling for fear of a sudden raid or attack by the agents of the state. It was that way under Muʿāwiyah[260] and similar rulers: people had no security, and they were killed or banished, or imprisoned for lengthy periods, on the strength of an accusation or a mere suspicion, because the government was not Islamic. When an Islamic government is established, all will live with complete security under the

---

[259] *Shāhi*: now obsolete, formerly the smallest unit of Iranian currency, worth one-twentieth of a rial.
[260] Muʿāwiyah: first of the Umayyad caliphs and an adversary of Imām ʿAli. He ruled from 41/661 to 60/680.

46

protection of the law, and no ruler will have the right to take any step contrary to the provisions and laws of the immaculate *sharī'ah*.

The meaning of "trustee," then, is that the *fuqahā* execute as a trust all the affairs for which Islam has legislated—not that they simply offer legal judgments on given questions. Was that the function of the Imām ('a)? Did he merely expound the law? Was it the function of the prophets ('a) from whom the *fuqahā* have inherited it as a trust? To offer judgment on a question of law or to expound the laws in general is, of course, one of the dimensions of *fiqh*. But Islam regards law as a tool, not as an end in itself. Law is a tool and an instrument for the establishment of justice in society, a means for man's intellectual and moral reform and his purification. Law exists to be implemented for the sake of establishing a just society that will morally and spiritually nourish refined human beings. The most significant duty of the prophets ('a) was the implementation of divine ordinances, and this necessarily involved supervision and rule.

There is a tradition of Imām Ridā ('a) in which he says approximately the following: "An upright, protecting, and trustworthy *imām* is necessary for the community in order to preserve it from decline," and then reasserts that the *fuqahā* are the trustees of the prophets ('a). Combining the two halves of the tradition, we reach the conclusion that the *fuqahā* must be the leaders of the people in order to prevent Islam from falling into decline and its ordinances from falling into abeyance.

Indeed it is precisely because the just *fuqahā* have not had executive power in the lands inhabited by Muslims and their governance has not been established that Islam has declined and its ordinances have fallen into abeyance. The words of Imām Ridā have fulfilled themselves; experience has demonstrated their truth.

Has Islam not declined? Have the laws of Islam not fallen into disused in the Islamic countries? The penal provisions of the law are not implemented; the ordinances of Islam are not enforced; the institutions of Islam have disappeared; chaos, anarchy, and confusion prevail—does not all this mean that Islam has declined? Is Islam simply something to be written down in books like *al-Kāfī*[261] and then laid aside? If the ordinances of Islam are not applied and the penal provisions of the law are not implemented in the external world—so that the thief, the plunderer, the oppressor, and the embezzler all go unpunished while we content ourselves with preserving the books of law, kissing them and laying them aside (even treating the Qur'an this way), and reciting *Yā-Sin* on Thursday nights[262]—can say that Islam has been preserved?

Since many of us did not really believe that Islamic society must be administered and ordered by an Islamic government matters have now reached such a state that in the Muslim countries, not only does the Islamic order not obtain, with corrupt and oppressive laws being implemented instead of the laws of Islam, but the provisions of Islam appear archaic even to the *'ulamā*. So when the subject is raised, they say that the tradition: "The *fuqahā* are trustees of the prophets" refers only to the issuing of juridical opinions. Ignoring the verses of the Qur'an, they distort in the same way all the numerous traditions that the scholars of Islam are to exercise rule during the Occultation. But can trusteeship be in this manner? Is the trustee not obliged to prevent the ordinances of Islam from falling into abeyance and criminals

---

[261] See n. 30 above.

[262] *Yā-Sin* is the thirty-sixth chapter of the Qur'an. Its recitation is recommended as particularly meritorious on certain occasions, among them Thursday night, because it leads into Friday, the best of all days.

from going unpunished? To prevent the revenue and income of the country from being squandered, embezzled or misdirected?

It is obvious that all of these tasks require the existence of trustees, and that it is the duty of the *fuqahā* to assume the trust bequeathed to them, to fulfill it in a just and trustworthy manner.

The Commander of the Faithful ('a) said to Shurayh[263]: "The seat [of judge] you are occupying is filled by someone who is a prophet ('a), the legatee of a prophet, or else a sinful wretch."[264] Now since Shurayh was neither a prophet nor the legatee of a prophet, it follows that he was a sinful wretch occupying the position of judge. Shurayh was a person who occupied the position of judge in Kūfah for about fifty or sixty years. Closely associated with the party of Mu'āwiyah, Shurayh spoke and issued *fatwās*[265] in a sense favorable to him, and he ended up rising in revolt against the Islamic state. The Commander of the Faithful ('a) was unable to dismiss Shurayh during his rule, because certain powerful figures protected him on the grounds that Abu Bakr and 'Umar had appointed him and that their action was not to be controverted. Shurayh was thus imposed upon the Commander of the Faithful ('a), who did, however, succeed in ensuring that he abided by the law in his judgment.

It is clear from the foregoing tradition that the position of judgment may be exercised only by a prophet ('a) or by the legatee of a prophet. No one would dispute the fact that the function of judge belongs to the just *fuqahā*, in accordance with their appointment by the Imāms ('a). This unanimity contrasts with the questions of the governance of the *faqīh*: some scholars, such as Narāqi,[266] or among more recent figures, Nā'ini,[267] regard all of the extrinsic functions and tasks of the Imāms ('a) as devolving upon the *faqih*, while other scholars do not. But there can be no doubt that the function of judging belongs to the just *fuqahā*; this is virtually self-evident.

Considering the fact that the *fuqahā* do not have the rank of prophethood, and they are indubitably not "wretched sinners," we conclude that, in the light of the tradition quoted above, they must be the legatees or successors of the Most Noble Messenger (s). Since, however, the expression "legatee of a prophet" is generally assumed to refer to his immediate successors, this tradition and others similar to it are only rarely cited as evidence for the successorship of the *fuqahā*. The concept "legatee of a prophet" is a broad one, however, and includes the *fuqahā*. The immediate legatee of the Most Noble Messenger (s) was of course the Commander of the Faithful ('a), who was followed by the other Imāms ('a), and the affairs of the people were entrusted to them. But no one should imagine that the function of governing or sitting in judgment was a form of privilege for the Imāms. Rule was entrusted to them only because they were best able to establish a just government and implement social

---

[263] Shurayh: more fully, Abū Umayyah Shurayh ibn al-Hārith al-Kindi, judge of Kūfah appointed by 'Umar. He retained this position under 'Uthmān, 'Ali, and the Umayyads and died a centenarian in 87/706. It is said that he sided with Ibn Ziyād and instigated the people against Imam Husayn in the 'Āshūrā uprising. [Pub.]

[264] From *Wasā'il ash-Shī'ah*, a Shī'i collection of traditions by Muhammad Hasan al-Hurr al-'Āmili (d. 1104/1693).

[265] *Fatwā*: the plural of *fatwā* (an authoritative opinion on a point of law).

[266] Narāqi: that is, Hājj Mullāh Ahmad Narāqi, a scholar of importance in the early nineteenth century, d. 1244/1829. He not only was a prolific author, but also clashed repeatedly with the monarch of his day, Fath 'Ali Shāh. See Hamid Algar, *Religion and State in Iran, 1785-1906* (Berkeley, 1969), pp. 57, 89.

[267] Nā'ini: that is, Mīrzā Muhammad Husayn Nā'ini, an important scholar of the early twentieth century, 1277/1860-1354/1936. Concerning his book on Shī'i political theory, *Tanbīh al-Ummah wa Tanzīh al-Millah*, see 'Abdul-Hādi Hā'iri, *Shi'ism and Constitutionalism in Iran* (Leiden, Netherlands, 1977), pp. 165-220.

justice among the people. The spiritual stations of the Imāms, which far transcend human comprehension, had no connection with their naming and appointing officials. If the Most Noble Messenger (s) had not appointed the Commander of the Faithful to be his successor, he would still have possessed the same sublime spiritual qualities. It is not that the exercise and function of government bestow spiritual rank and privilege on a man; on the contrary, spiritual rank and privilege qualify a man for the assumption of government and social responsibilities.

In any event, we deduce from the tradition quoted above that the *fuqahā* are the legatees, at one remove, of the Most Noble Messenger (s) and that all the tasks he entrusted to the Imāms ('a) are also incumbent on the *fuqahā*; all the tasks that Messenger (s) performed, they too must perform, just as the Commander of the Faithful ('a) did.

There is another tradition that may serve as proof or support for our thesis, one that is, indeed, preferable with respect to both its chain of transmission and its meaning. One chain of transmission for it, that passing through Kulayni, is weak, but the other, mentioned by Sadūq and passing through Sulaymān ibn Khālid[108a] is authentic and reliable. This is the text of the tradition. Imām Ja'far as-Sādiq[268] ('a) said: "Refrain from judging, because judging is reserved for an *imām* who is knowledgeable of the law and legal procedures and who behaves justly toward all the Muslims; it is reserved for a prophet ('a) or the legatee of a prophet."

Notice that the person who wishes to sit in judgment must, first of all, be an *imām*. What is meant here by *imām* is the common lexical meaning of the word, "leader" or "guide," not its specific technical sense. In this context the Prophet (s) himself counts as an *imām*. If the technical meaning of *imām*[269] were intended, the specification of the attributes of justice and knowledge in the tradition would be superfluous. Second, the person who wishes to exercise the function of a judge must possess the necessary knowledge. If he is an *imām*, but unlearned in matters of law and juridical procedure, he does not have the right to be a judge. Third, he must be just. The position of judge, then, is reserved for those who posses these three qualifications—being a leader, and being knowledgeable and just. The tradition proceeds to clarify that these three qualifications can be found only in a prophet ('a) or the trustee of a prophet.

I stated earlier that the function of judge belongs exclusively to the just *faqīh*; this is a fundamental aspect of *fiqh*, which is not a matter of dispute. Let us now see whether the three-fold qualifications for exercising the function of judge are present in the *faqīh*. Obviously we are concerned here only with the just *faqīh*, not with any *faqīh*. The *faqīh* is, by definition, learned in matters pertaining to the function of judge, since the term *faqīh* is applied to one who is learned not only in the laws and judicial procedure of Islam, but also in the doctrines, institutions, and ethics of the faith—the *faqīh* is, in short, a religious expert in the full sense of the word. If, in addition, the *faqīh* is just, he will be found to have two of the necessary qualifications. The third qualification is that he should be an imām, in the sense of leader. Now we

---

[108a] Sulaymān ibn Khālid: more fully, Sulaymān ibn Khālid ibn Dehqān ibn Nāfilah, was a reciter, jurist, traditionist, and a trustee and confidant of Imāms al-Bāqir and as-Sāqid ('a). [Pub.]

[268] Imām Ja'far as-Sādiq: sixth of the Twelve Imāms, 83/702-140/757. Also referred to as Imām Sādiq, he was particularly important for his role in developing the religious sciences. See Shaykh Mohammed al-Husayn al-Muzaffar, *Imām Al-Sādiq*, trans. Jāsim al-Rasheed (Qum: Ansariyan Publications, 1998). [Pub.]

[269] The technical sense of the word *imām* is that which it requires when applied to the Twelve Imāms, who were not only successors to the Prophet but also endowed with lofty spiritual virtues.

have already stated that the just *faqīh* occupies a position of guidance and leadership with respect to judging, in accordance with his appointment by the Imām ('a). Further, the Imām has specified that the three necessary qualifications are not to be found in anyone except a prophet ('a) or the legatee of a prophet. Since the *fuqahā* are not prophets ('a) they must be legatees or successors of the prophets ('a). Therefore, we come to the conclusion that the *faqīh* is the legatee of the Most Noble Messenger (s), and in addition, during the Occultation of the Imām ('a), he is the leader of the Muslims and the chief of the community. He alone may exercise the function of judge and no one else has the right to occupy the position of judgeship.

To whom should we recourse in social circumstances?

The third tradition relates to a signed decree of the Imām from which certain conclusions may be deduced, as I propose to do.

It is related in the book *Ikmāl ad-Dīn wa Itmām an-Ni'mah*[270] that Ishāq ibn Ya'qūb wrote a letter to the Imām of the Age[271] (may God hasten his renewed manifestation) asking him for guidance in certain problems that had arisen, and Muhammad ibn 'Uthmān al-'Umari,[272] the deputy of the Imām ('a), conveyed the letter to him. A response was issued, written in the blessed hand of the Imam ('a), saying: "In case of newly occurring social circumstances, you should turn for guidance to those who relate our traditions, for they are my proof to you, as I am God's proof."

What is meant here by the phrase "newly occurring social circumstances" (*hawādith-i wāqi'ah*) is not legal cases and ordinances. The writer of the letter did not wish to ask what was to be done in the case of legal issues that were without precedent. For the answer to that question would have been self-evident according to the Shī'i school, and unanimously accepted traditions specify that one should have recourse to the *fuqahā* in such cases. Indeed people had recourse to the *fuqahā* and made enquiries of them even during the lifetime of the Imāms ('a). A person living in the time of the Lesser Occultation and in communication with the four deputies of the Imam ('a), who wrote a letter to him and received an answer, must have known whom to refer to for the solution of legal cases. What is meant by *hawādith-i wāqi'ah* is rather the newly arising situations and problems that affect the people and the Muslims. The question Ishāq ibn Ya'qūb was implicitly posing was this: "Now that we no longer have access to you, what should we do with respect to social problems? What is our duty?" Or, he may have mentioned certain specific events and then asked: "To whom should we have recourse for guidance in these matters?" But it seems that his question was general in intent and that the Imām ('a) responded in correspondingly general fashion, saying, "With respect to such occurrences and problems, you should refer to those who narrate our traditions, i.e., the *fuqahā*. They are my proofs to you, and I am God's proof to you."

What is the meaning of "God's proof"?[273] What do you understand by this term? Can a single tradition count as a proof? If Zurārah[274] related a tradition, would

---

[270] *Ikmāl ad-Dīn wa Itmām an-Ni'mah*: a work by Shaykh Sadūq on the occultation of the Imām.

[271] Imām of the Age: the Twelfth Imām. See n. 95 above.

[272] Muhammad ibn 'Uthmān al-'Umari: the second deputy of the Imām during the Lesser Occultation. See n. 27 above.

[273] The designation *hujjat* ("proof") given to the Imāms has a two-fold sense. First, through the qualities they manifest, they are proofs of the existence of God and of the veracity of the religion He has revealed. Second, they constitute proofs to be advanced on the Day of Judgment against those who claim they were uninformed of God's law. See 'Abdul 'Azīz 'Abdulhussein Sachedina, *Islamic Messianism* (Albany, N.Y., 1980), pp. 66-67.

that make him a proof? Is the Imām of the Age ('a) comparable in authority to Zurārah, whom we follow in the sense that we act upon a tradition of the Most Noble Messenger (s) that Zurārah has narrated? When it is said that the holder of authority is the proof of God, does it mean that he is a "proof" purely with respect to details of the law, with the duty of giving legal opinions? The Most Noble Messenger (s) said: "I am now departing, and the Commander of the Faithful ('a) will be my proof to you." Do you deduce from this that after the Prophet (s) departed all tasks came to an end except delivering legal opinions, and that this was all that was left for the Commander of the Faithful ('a)? Or on the contrary, does the term "proof of God" mean that just as the Most Noble Messenger (s) was the proof and authoritative guide of all the people, just as God had appointed him to guide people in matters, so too the *fuqahā* are responsible for all affairs and are the authoritative guides of the people?

A "proof of God" is one whom God has designated to conduct affairs; all his deeds, actions, and sayings constitute a proof for the Muslims. If some one commits an offense, reference will be to the "proof" for adducing evidence and formulating the charge. If the "proof" commands you to perform a certain act, to implement the penal provisions of the law in a certain way, or to spend the income derived from booty, *zakāt*, and *sadaqah*[275] in a certain manner, and you fail to obey him in any of these respects, then God Almighty will advance a "proof" against you on the Day of Judgment. If, despite the existence of the "proof," you turn to oppressive authorities for the solution of your affairs, again God Almighty will refer to the "proof" as an argument against you on the Day of Judgment, saying: "I established a proof for you; why did you turn instead to the oppressors and the judicial system of the wrongdoers?" Similarly, God designates the Commander of the Faithful ('a) as a "proof" against those who disobeyed him and followed false paths. Again, against those who assumed the caliphate, against Mu'āwiyah and the Umayyad caliphs, against the Abbasid caliphs, and those who acted in accordance with their desires, a proof and argument is established: "Why did you illicitly assume rule over the Muslims? Why did you usurp the caliphate and government, despite your unworthiness?"

God calls to account all oppressive rulers and all governments that act contrary to the criteria of Islam, asking them: "Why did you commit oppression? Why did you squander the property of the Muslims? Why did you organize millenary celebrations?[276] Why did you spend the wealth of the people on the coronation[277] and the abominable festivities that accompanied it?" If one of them should reply: "Given the circumstances of the day, I was unable to act justly, or to relinquish my pretentious, luxurious palaces; I had myself crowned to draw attention to my country and the degree of progress we had achieved," he will then be answered: "The Commander of the Faithful ('a) was also a ruler; he ruled over all the Muslims and the whole of the broad Islamic realm. Were you more zealous than he in promoting the glory of Islam, the Muslims and the lands of Islam? Was your realm more extensive

---

[274] Zurārah: more fully, 'Abd Rabbih ibn A'yan Shaybāni al-Kufi al-Zurārah, an authority on the traditions of the fourth, fifth, and sixth Imāms, d. 150/767. Scholars of *'ilm ar-rijāl* (science of *hadīth* transmitters' biographies) have affirmed his reliability. He was known to have authored the books *Al-Istitā'ah* and *Al-Jabr*. [Pub.]

[275] *Sadaqah*: voluntary payments collected by the Muslim state to be spent for purposes of charity.

[276] The Shāh organized his vulgar and criminally extravagant celebration of two-and-a-half millennia of monarchical rule in October 1971, some two years after these lectures were given in Najaf. Preparations for the event, however, were begun in the late 1960's. See also *Islam and Revolution*, pp. 200-208.

[277] In 1967 the Shāh had himself and his wife crowned.

51

than his? The country over which you ruled was but a part of his realm; Iraq, Egypt and the Hijāz all belonged to his realm, as well as Iran. Despite this, his seat of command was the mosque: the bench of the judge was situated in one corner of the mosque, while in another, the army would prepare to set out for battle. That army was composed of people who offered their prayers regularly, were firm believers in Islam; you know well how swiftly it advanced and what results it obtained!"

Today, the *fuqahā* of Islam are proof to the people. Just as the Most Noble Messenger (ʿa) was the proof of God---the conduct of all affairs was entrusted to him so that whoever disobeyed him had a proof advanced against him---so, too, the *fuqahā* are the proof of the Imām (ʿa) to the people. All the affairs of the Muslims have been entrusted to them. God will advance a proof and argument against anyone who disobeys them in anything concerning government, the conduct of Muslim affairs, or the gathering and expenditure of public funds.

There can be no doubt concerning the meaning of the tradition we have quoted, although it is possible to have certain reservations about its chain transmission. Nonetheless, even if one does regard the tradition as being in its own right, a proof of the thesis we have advanced, it serves to support the other proofs we have mentioned.

Another tradition that supports our thesis is the *maqbūlah*[278] of ʿUmar ibn Hanzalah. Since this narration refers to a certain verse of the Qurʾan, we must first discuss the verse in question as well as the verses that precede it in order to elucidate its meaning, before we go on to examine the tradition. I seek refuge in Allah, from the accursed Satan.

In the name of God, the Compassionate, the Merciful.

Verily God commands you to return trusts to their owners, and to act with justice when you rule among men. Verily, God counsels you thus, and God is all hearing, all seeing. O you who believe, obey God and obey the Messenger and the holders of authority from among you [i.e., those entrusted with leadership and government]. When you dispute with each other concerning a thing, refer it to God and His Messenger; if you believe in God and the Last Day, this will be best for you and the result, most beneficial. (4: 58-59)

In these verses, God commands us to return trusts to their owners. Some people believe that what is meant here by "trusts" is twofold: trust pertaining to men (i.e., their property), and those pertaining to the Creator (i.e., the ordinances of the *sharīʿah*).[279] The sense of returning the divine trust would then be implementing the ordinances of Islam correctly and completely. Another group of exegetes believes instead that what is intended by "trust" is the imamate.[280] There is indeed a tradition that specifies: "We [the Imāms (ʿa)] are those addressed in this verse," for God Almighty commands the Most Noble Messenger (s) and the Imāms to entrust governance and leadership to their rightful possessors. Thus the Most Noble Messenger (s) entrusted governance to the Commander of the Faithful (ʿa), who entrusted it to his successor, and each of his successors among the Imāms (ʿa) handed it on in turn.

The verse goes on to say: "and to act with justice when you rule among men." Those addressed here are the person who hold the reins of affairs in their hands and conduct the business of government—not judges, for the judge exercises only a

---

[278] *Maqbūlah*: a *hadīth* to which one may make acceptable reference.
[279] See, for example, Ismāʿīl Haqqi al-Burūsawi, *Ruh al-Bayān* (Istanbul, 1390/1970), II, 227-228.
[280] See, for example, Tabātabāʾi, *al-Mīzān*, IV, 385.

juridical function, not a governmental one. The judge is a ruler only in a limited sense; the decrees that he issues are exclusively judicial, not executive. Indeed, in forms of government that have emerged in recent centuries, the judges represent one of the three branches of power, the other two being the executive (consisting of the council of ministers) and the legislative or planning body (the assembly or parliament). More generally, the judiciary is one of the branches of government and it fulfills one of the tasks of government. We must therefore conclude that the phrase "when you rule among men" relates to all the affairs of government, and includes both judges and those belonging to the other branches of power.

Now it has been established that since all the concerns of religion constitute a divine trust; a trust that must be vested in its rightful possessors a part of the trust must inevitably be government. Thus, in accordance with this verse, the conduct of all governmental affairs must be based on the criteria of justice, or to put it differently, on the law of Islam and the ordinances of the *sharī'ah*. The judge may not issue an incorrect verdict—i.e., one based on some illegitimate, non-Islamic code—nor may the judicial procedure he follows or the law on which he bases his verdict be non-Islamic and therefore invalid. For example, when those engaged in planning the affairs of the country draw up a fiscal program for the nation, they must not impose unjust taxes on peasants working on publicly owned lands, reducing them to wretchedness and destroying the land and agriculture as a whole through the burden of excessive taxation. If the executive branch of government wishes to implement the juridical ordinances of the law and its penal provisions, they must not go beyond the limits of the law by inflicting extra lashes upon the offender or abusing him.

After the Commander of the Faithful ('a) had cut off the hands of two thieves, he showed such love and concern in treating them and attending to their needs that they became his enthusiastic supporters. On another occasion, he heard that the plundering army of Mu'āwiyah had stolen an anklet from the foot of a *dhimmi*[281] woman. He became so distraught and his sensibilities were so offended that he said in a speech: "If a person were to die in circumstances such as mine, no one would reproach him." But despite all this sensitivity, the Commander of the Faithful ('a) was a man who would draw his sword when it was necessary—to destroy the workers of corruption—with all the strength he could muster. This is the true meaning of justice.

The Most Noble Messenger (s) is the foremost example of the just ruler. When he gave orders for the conquest of a certain area, the burning of a certain place, or the destruction of a certain group whose existence was harmful for Islam, the Muslims, and mankind in general, his orders were just. If he had not given orders such as these, it would have meant neglecting the welfare of Islam, the Muslims, and human society.

Anyone who rules over the Muslims, or over human society in general, must always take into consideration, the public welfare and interest, and ignore personal feelings and interests. For this reason, Islam is prepared to subordinate individuals to the collective interest of society and has rooted out numerous groups that were a source of corruption and harm to human society.

Since the Jews of Bani Qurayza were a troublesome group, causing corruption in Muslim society and damaging Islam and the Islamic state, the Most Noble Messenger ('a) eliminated them.[282]

---

[281] *Dhimmi*: one of the *ahl adh-dhimmi*, concerning whom see n. 35 above.

[282] The Bani Qurayza was a Jewish tribe inhabiting Medina. During the Battle of the Ditch (*Ghazwat al-Khandaq*) in the fifth year of Islam, they collaborated with a Meccan force that came to attack the city. The menfolk of the tribe were put to death for their treachery. See chapter 38, "The Last Stage of Mischief," of Āyatullāh Ja'far Subhāni's *The Message* (Karachi: Islamic Seminary Publications) [Pub.]

Indeed, there are two essential qualities in a believer: he executes justice whenever necessary, with the utmost force and decisiveness and without exhibiting the least trace of feeling; and he displays the utmost love and solicitude whenever they are called for. In these two ways, the believer comes to serve as a refuge for society. Society, with both Muslim and non-Muslim members, will achieve security and tranquility as the result of government exercised by believers, and everybody will live in ease and without fear. The fact that men in our age live in fear of their rulers is because existing governments are not based on law; they are a form of banditry. But in the case of a government headed by someone like the Commander of the Faithful ('a), that is, in the case of an Islamic government, only the traitors and oppressors—those who transgress and encroach on the rights of their fellows—suffer fear; for the public at large, fear and anxiety are nonexistent.

In the second of the two verses we have quoted, God Almighty says: "O you who believe, obey God and obey the Messenger and the holders of authority among you" (4:59).

According to a certain tradition, the beginning of the first verse ("return trusts to their owners") is addressed to the Imāms ('a), the next part of that verse, concerning rule with justice, is addressed to those who exercise command, and the second verse ("O you who believe...") is addressed to the entire Muslim people. God commands them to obey Him by following his divine ordinances, and to obey His Most Noble Messenger (s) as well as the holders of authority (i.e., the Imāms) by adhering to their teachings and following their governmental decrees.

I have already said that obedience to the commands of God Almighty is different from obedience to the Most Noble Messenger (s). All the ordinances of divine law, whether or not they relate to worship, are the commands of God and to implement them is to obey God. The Most Noble Messenger (s) did not issue any commands concerning prayer, and if he urged men to pray, it was by way of confirming and implementing God's command. When we pray, we too are obeying God; obeying the Messenger is different from obeying God.

The commands of the Most Noble Messenger (s) are those that he himself issued in the course of exercising his governmental function, as when, for example, he commanded the Muslims to follow the army of Usāmah,[283] to protect the frontiers of the Islamic state in certain way, to levy taxes on certain categories of people, and in general to interact with people in certain prescribed ways. All of these were commands of the Prophet (s). God has laid upon us the duty of obeying the Messenger (s). It is also our duty to follow and obey the holders of authority, who, according to our beliefs, are the Imāms ('a). Of course, obedience to their governmental decrees is also a form of obedience to God. Since God Almighty has commanded us to follow the Messenger (s) and the holders of authority, our obeying them is actually an expression of obedience to God.

The verse we have cited continues: "When you dispute with each other concerning a thing, refer it to God and His Messenger." Disputes that arise among people are of two kinds. First, there is the dispute arising between two groups or two individuals concerning a particular matter or claim. For example, someone may claim that there is a debt owed him, while the order party denies it; the truth of the matter must then be established, in accordance either with the *sharī'ah* or with customary

---

[283] Usāmah: see n. 98 above.

law.[284] In such cases one must turn to judges, who will examine the matter and deliver an appropriate verdict. The first kind of dispute then, is a civil one.

The second kind of dispute does not concern a disagreement of this type, but relates to oppression and crime. If a robber takes someone's property by force, for example, or makes illicit use of people's property, or if a burglar inters someone's house and carries off his property, the competent authority to whom one should have recourse is not the judge but the public prosecutor. In such matters as this, which relates to penal not civil law (apart from some cases, which are simultaneously civil and penal), it is primarily the public prosecutor who is the guardian of the law and its ordinances and the protector of society. He begins his task by issuing an indictment, and then the judge examines the matter and delivers a verdict. The verdicts issued, whether civil or penal in nature, are put into effect by another branch of power, the executive.

The Qur'an says, then, in effect: "Whenever a dispute arises among you concerning any matter, your point of reference must be God and His ordinances and the Messenger (s), the executor of those ordinances. The Messenger (s) must receive the ordinances from God and implement them. If any dispute arises among you concerning a debt or loan, the Messenger (s) will intervene in his capacity as judge and deliver a verdict. If other disputes arise involving unlawful coercion or the usurpation of rights, again it is to the Prophet (s) that you should have recourse. Since he is the head of the Islamic state, he is obliged to enact justice. He must dispatch an official whose duty is to recover the usurped right and restore it to its owner. Further, in any matter where people had recourse to the Messenger, recourse must be to the Imāms, and obedience to the Imāms is, in effect, obedience to the Most Noble Messenger (s)."

In short, both of these verses with all their components embrace government in general, as well as judgehood; they are not restricted in any way to the function of judging, quiet aside from the consideration that certain verses of the Qur'an explicitly relate to government in the sense of the executive.

In the next verse, God says: "Have you not looked at those who claim to believe in what was revealed to you and what was revealed before you? They wish to seek justice from tāghūt [illegitimate powers], even though they have been commanded to disbelieve in therein" (4:60). Even if we do not interpret tāghūt as oppressive governments and all illicit forms of power that have revolted against divine government in order to establish monarchy or some other form of rule, we must still interpret it as including both judges and rulers. For customarily, one has recourse to the judicial authorities to initiate legal proceedings and obtain redress and the punishment of the offender, but then, the juridical verdict that they reach must be implemented by the executive power, which usually forms a separate branch of the government. Tyrannical governments—including the judiciary, the executives, and all other components of the state—comprise what is meant by tāghūt, for they have rebelled against divine command by instituting evil laws, implementing them, and then making them the basis of judicial practice. God has commanded us to disbelieve in them; that is, to revolt against them and their commands and ordinances. All who wish to disbelieve, in this sense, in the tāghūt —that is, to rise up in disobedience against illegitimate ruling powers —have a formidable duty that they must strive to fulfill as far as they are able.

---

[284] The reference to customary law ('urf) is not intended to sanction, but merely to clarify, existing judicial practice.

Now let us examine the tradition known as the *maqbūlah* of ʿUmar ibn Hanzalah to establish its meaning and intent. ʿUmar ibn Hanzalah says: "I asked Imām as-Sādiq (ʿa) whether it was permissible for two of the Shīʿah who had a disagreement concerning a dept or a legacy to seek the verdict of the ruler or judge. He replied: 'Any one who has recourse to the ruler or judge, whether his case be just or unjust, has in reality had recourse to *tāghūt* [i.e. the illegitimate ruling power]. Whatever he obtains as result of their verdict, he will have obtained by forbidden means, even if he has a proven right to it, for he will have obtained it through the verdict and judgment of the *tāghūt*, that power which God Almighty has commanded him to disbelieve in.'" ("They wish to seek justice from illegitimate powers, even though they have been commanded to disbelieve therein" [4:60].)

ʿUmar ibn Hanzalah then asked: "What should these two Shīʿah do then, under such circumstances?" Imām as-Sādiq (ʿa) answered: "They must seek out one of you who narrates our tradition, who is versed in what is permissible and what is forbidden, who is well acquainted with our laws and ordinances, and accept him as judge and arbiter, for I appoint him as judge over you."[285]

As both the beginning and the conclusion of this tradition make clear, and also the reference made by the Imām (ʿa) to the Qurʾanic verse, the scope of the question put to the Imām was general, and the instructions he gave in response were also of general validity. I said earlier that for the adjudication of both civil and penal cases, one must have recourse to judges, as well as to the executive authorities or general governmental authorities. One has recourse to judges in order to establish the truth, reconcile enmities, or determine punishments; and to the executive authorities, in order to obtain compliance with the verdict given by the judge and the enactment of his verdict, whether the case is civil or penal in nature. It is for reason that in the tradition under discussion the Imām (ʿa) was asked whether we may have recourse to the existing rulers and powers, together with their judicial apparatus.

In his answer, the Imām (ʿa) condemns all recourse to illegitimate governments, including both their executive and their judicial branches. He forbids the Muslims to have recourse in any of their affairs to kings and tyrannical rulers, as well as to the judges who act as their agents, even if they have some well-established right that they wish to have enforced. Even if a Muslim's son has been killed or his house has been ransacked, he does not have the right of recourse to oppressive rulers in order to obtain justice. Similarly, if a debt is owed to him and he has irrefutable evidence to that effect, again he may not have recourse to judges who are the servants and appointees of oppressors. If a Muslim does have recourse to them in such cases and obtains his undeniable rights by means of those illegitimate powers and authorities, the result he obtains will be *harām*,[286] and he will have no right to make use of it. Certain *fuqahā* have even gone so far as to say that, in cases where property is restored, the same rule applies. For example, if your cloak is stolen from you, and you regain it through the intervention of an illegitimate authority, you have no right to wear it. This particular ruling is open to discussion, but there is no doubt in more general cases. For example, if someone has a debt owed to him, and, in order to obtain it, has recourse to a body or authority other than that specified by God, and he subsequently receives his due, he may not legitimately put it to use. The fundamental criteria of the *sharīʿah* make this necessary.

---

[285] This tradition is contained in al-ʾĀmili, *Wasāʾil ash-Shīʿah*, XVII, 98.

[286] *Harām*: categorically forbidden by religious law.

So this is the political ruling of Islam. It is a ruling that makes Muslims refrain from having recourse to illegitimate powers and their appointed judges, so that non-Islamic and oppressive regimes may fall and the top-heavy judicial systems that produce nothing for the people but trouble may be abolished. This, in turn would open the way for having recourse to the Imāms ('a) and those to whom they have assigned the right to govern and judge. The main purpose was to prevent kings and the judges appointed by them from attaining any form of authority, and people not to follow them. It has been declared to the Islamic nation that they are not authorities whom to be referred for God Himself had commanded men to disbelieve in kings and unjust rulers (i.e., to rebel against them),[287] and to have recourse to them would conflict with this duty. If you disbelieve in them and regard them as oppressors who are unfit to rule you must not have recourse to them.

What then is the duty of the Islamic community in this respect? What are they to do when new problems occur and dispute arises among them? To what authority should they have recourse? In the tradition previously quoted, the Imām ('a) said: "They must seek out one of you who narrates our traditions, who is versed in what is permissible and what is forbidden"—that is, whenever disputes arise among them, they should seek to have them resolved by those who narrate our *hadith*, are acquainted with what God has made permissible or forbidden, and comprehend our ordinances in accordance with the criteria of reason and the *sharī'ah*. The Imām ('a) did not leave any room for ambiguity lest someone say: "So, scholars of traditions are also to act as authorities and judges." The Imām ('a) mentioned all the necessary qualifications and specified that the person to whom we have recourse must be able to give an opinion concerning what is permissible and forbidden in accordance with the well-known rules, must be knowledgeable with the ordinances of Islam, and must be aware of the criteria needed to identify the traditions originating in *taqiyyah* or similar circumstances (which are not to be taken as valid). It is obvious that such knowledge of the ordinances of Islam and expertise in the science of tradition is different from mere ability to narrate tradition.

In the same tradition the Imām ('a) goes on to say: "I appoint him as ruler over you"—that is, "I appoint as ruler over you one who possesses such qualifications; I appoint anyone who possesses them to conduct the governmental and judicial affairs of the Muslims, and the Muslims do not have the right to have recourse to anyone other than him." Therefore, if a robber steals your property, you should bring your complaint to the authorities appointed by the Imām ('a). If you have a dispute with someone concerning debt or a loan and you need the truth of the matter to be established, again you should refer the matter to the judge appointed by the Imām ('a), and not to anyone else. This is the universal duty of all Muslims, not simply of 'Umar ibn Hanzalah, who, when confronted by a particular problem, obtained the ruling.

This decree issued by the Imām ('a), then, is general and universal in scope. For just as the Commander of the Faithful ('a), while he exercised rule, appointed governors and judges whom all Muslims were bound to obey, so, too, Imām as-Sādiq ('a), holding absolute authority and empowerment to rule over all the *'ulamā*, the *fuqahā*, and the people at large, was able to appoint rulers and judges not only for his own lifetime, but also for subsequent ages. This indeed he did, naming the *fuqahā* as "rulers," so that no one might presume that their function was restricted to judicial affairs and divorced from the other concerns of government.

---

[287] See Qur'an, 2:256.

57

We may also deduce from the beginning and end of this tradition, as well as from the Qur'anic verse to which it refers, that the Imām ('a) was not concerned simply with the appointing of judges and did not leave other duties of the Muslims unclarified, for otherwise, one of the two questions posed to him—that concerned with seeking justice from illicit executive authorities—would have remained unanswered.

This tradition is perfectly clear; there are no doubts surrounding its chain of transmission or its meaning. No one can doubt that the Imām ('a) designated the *fuqahā* to exercise the functions of both government and judgeship. It is the duty of all Muslims to obey this decree of the Imām ('a).

In order to clarify the matter still further, I will adduce additional traditions, beginning with that of Abū Khadījah.

Abū Khadījah, one of the trusted companions of Imām as-Sādiq ('a), relates: "I was commanded by the Imām ('a) to convey the following message to our friends [i.e., the Shī'ah]: 'When enmity and dispute arise among you, or you disagree concerning the receipt or payment of a sum of money, be sure not to refer the matter to one of these malefactors for judgment. Designate as judge and arbiter someone among you who is acquainted with our injunctions concerning what is permitted and what is prohibited, for I appoint such a man as judge over you. Let none of you take your complaint against another of you to the tyrannical ruling power.' "[288]

The meaning of the phrase "dispute concerning a thing" relates to civil disputes, so that the first part of the Imām's decree means that we are not to have recourse to the malefactors. Concerning part of the tradition which says "I appoint such a man as judge over you" it becomes clear that 'malefactors' means those judges whom the rulers of the day and illegitimate governments have allowed to occupy the position of judge. The Imām ('a) goes on to say "Let none of you take your complaint against another of you to the tyrannical ruling power." That is to say, "Whatever personal disputes arise among you, do not have recourse to tyrannical authorities and illegitimate powers; do not seek their aid in matters relating to the executive." The expression "tyrannical ruler" refers, in general, to all illegitimate powers and authorities (that is, all non-Islamic rulers) and embraces all three branches of government—judicial, legislative and executive. Considering that earlier in the tradition, recourse to tyrannical judges is prohibited, however, it appears that this second prohibition relates to the executive branch. The final sentence is not a repetition of the preceding statement. First, the Imām prohibits having recourse to impious judges in the various matters that are their concern (interrogation, the establishment of proof, and so on), designates those who may act as judge, and clarifies the duties of his followers. Then he declares that they must refrain from having recourse to illegitimate rulers. This makes it plain that the question of judges is separate from that of having recourse to illegitimate authority; they are two different subjects. Both are mentioned in the tradition of 'Umar ibn Hanzalah; there, the seeking of justice from both illegitimate authorities and judges is forbidden. In the tradition of Abū Khadijah the Imām ('a) has appointed only judges, but in that reported by 'Umar ibn Hanzalah the Imām ('a) has designated both those who are to act as ruler and executive and those who are to act as judge.

In accordance with the tradition narrated Abu Khadijah, then, the Imām ('a) designated the *fuqahā* as judges in his own lifetime, and according to that narrated by 'Umar ibn Hanzalah, he assigned them both governmental and judicial authority. We must now examine whether the *fuqahā* automatically forfeited those functions when

---

[288] See al-'Āmili, *Wasā'il ash-Shī'ah*, XVIII, 100.

the Imām ('a) left this world? Were all the judges and rulers appointed by the Imāms ('a) somehow dismissed from their functions when the Imāms ('a) left?

The governance of the Imāms ('a) differs, of course, from that of all others; according to the Shi'ah school, all the commands and instructions of the Imāms ('a) must be obeyed, both during their lifetime and after their death. But, aside from this consideration, let us see what becomes of the functions and duties they have assigned in this world to the *fuqahā*.

In all existing forms of government whether monarchical, republican, or following some other model, if the head of state dies or circumstances change so that there is a change in administration, military ranks and appointments are not affected. For example, a general will not automatically be deprived of his rank, an ambassador will not be dismissed from his post, and a minister of finance or a provincial or local governor will not be removed. The new administration or successor administration may, of course, dismiss or transfer them from their posts, but their functions are not automatically withdrawn from them.

Obviously, certain powers do automatically terminate with death of the person who conferred them. Such is the case with *ijāza-yi hasbiyyah*, the authority given to someone by a *faqīh* to fulfill certain tasks on his behalf in a given town; when the *faqīh* dies, this authority expires. But, in another case, if a *faqīh* appoints a guardian for a minor or a trustee for an endowment, the appointments he makes are not annulled by his death but continue in force.

The judicial and governmental functions assigned by the Imāms to the *fuqahā* of Islam are retained permanently. The Imām ('a) was certainly aware of all aspects of the matter, and there can be no possibility of carelessness on his part. He must have known that in all governments of the world the position and authority of individual officeholders is not affected by the death or departure of the head of state. If he had intended that the right to govern and judge should be withdrawn after his death from the *fuqahā* whom he had designated, he would have specified that to be the case, saying: "The *fuqahā* are to exercise these functions as long as I live."

According to this tradition, then, the '*ulamā* of Islam have been appointed by the Imām ('a) to the positions of ruler and judge, and these positions belong to them in perpetuity. The possibility that the next Imām would have annulled this decree and dismissed the *fuqahā* from these twin functions is extremely small. For the Imām forbade the Muslims to have recourse to kings and their appointed judges for obtaining their rights, and designated recourse to them as equivalent to recourse to the *tāghūt*; then, referring to the verse that ordains disbelief in *tāghūt*,[289] he appointed legitimate judges and rulers for the people. If his successor as Imām were not to have assigned the same functions to the *fuqahā* or to the new ones, what should the Muslims have done, and how would they have resolved their differences and disputes? Should they have had recourse to sinners and oppressors, which would have been equivalent to recourse to the *tāghūt* and thus a violation of divine command? Or should they have had recourse to no one at all, depriving themselves of all authority and refuge, which would have allowed anarchy to take over, with people freely usurping each other's property, transgressing against each other's rights, and being completely unrestrained in all they did?

We are certain that if Imām as-Ṣādiq ('a) assigned these functions to the *fuqahā*, neither his son Mūsā ('a) nor any of the succeeding Imāms ('a) abrogated them. Indeed, it is not possible for them to have abrogate these functions and said:

---

[289] Here, "disbelief" implies disobedience. See p. 92.

"Henceforth, do not have recourse to the just *fuqahā* for the settlement of your affairs; instead, turn to kings, or do nothing at all and allow your rights to be trampled underfoot."

Naturally, if an Imām appoints a judge to a certain city, his successor may dismiss that judge and appoint another in his place, but the positions and functions that have been established cannot themselves be abolished. That is self-evident.

The tradition that I shall now quote supports the thesis I have been advancing. If the only proof I had were one of the traditions I have been citing, I would be unable to substantiate my claim. Its essence, however, has been proved by the traditions already cited; what follows now is by way of supplementary evidence. Imām as-Sādiq ('a) relates that the Prophet (s) said: "For whomever travels a path in search of knowledge, God opens up a path to paradise, and the angels lower their wings before him as a sign of their being well pleased [or God's being well pleased]. All that is in the heavens and on earth, even the fish in the ocean, seeks forgiveness for him. The superiority of the learned man over the mere worshipper is like that of the full moon over the stars. Truly the scholars are the heirs of prophets ('a); the prophets bequeathed not a single dinār or dirham; instead they bequeathed knowledge, and whoever acquires it has indeed acquired a generous portion of their legacy."[290]

The links in the chain of transmission of this tradition are all trustworthy; in fact, Ibrāhīm ibn Hāshim, father of 'Ali ibn Ibrāhīm, is not moderately trustworthy but outstandingly so. The same tradition has been narrated with a slightly different text by another chain of transmission, one that is sound as far as Abū 'l-Bukhtūri although Abū'l-Bukhtūri himself is of questionable reliability. Here is the second version of the tradition: "Muhammad ibn Yahyā relates, on the authority of Ahmad ibn Muhammad ibn Īsā, who was told it by Muhammad ibn Khālid, to whom it was narrated by Abū 'l- Bukhtūri, that Imām Ja'far as-Sādiq ('a) said: 'The scholars are the heirs of the prophets, for although the prophets bequeathed not a single dinār or dirham, they bequeathed their sayings and traditions. Whoever, then, acquires a portion of their traditions has indeed acquired a generous portion of their legacy. Therefore, see from whom you may acquire this knowledge, for among us, the Family of the Prophet, there are in each generation just and honest people who will repel those who distort and exaggerate, those who initiate false practices, and those who offer foolish interpretations [that is, they will purify and protect religion from the influence of such biased and ignorant people and others like them].' "[291]

Our purpose in citing this tradition (which has also been referred to by the late Narāqi) is that it clarifies the meaning of the expression: "The scholars are the heirs of the prophets." There are several matters that must be explained at this point.

First, who are "the scholars"? Is it intended to mean the scholars of the Muslim community or the Imāms ('a)? Some people are of the opinion probably the Imāms are intended. But it would appear that, on the contrary, the scholars of the community—the *'ulamā*—are intended. The tradition itself indicates this, for the virtues and qualities of the Imāms ('a) that have mentioned elsewhere are quite different from what this tradition contains. The statement that the prophets ('a) have bequeathed traditions and whoever learns those traditions acquires a generous portion of their legacy cannot serve as a definition of the Imāms. It must therefore refer to the scholars of the community. In addition, in the version narrated by Abū 'l-Bukhtūri, after the phrase: "The scholars are the heirs of the prophets," we read: "Therefore, see

---

[290] This tradition is quoted in Kulayni, *al-Kāfi*, I, ii, 85-86.

[291] Kulayni, *al-Kāfi*, I, 78-79.

from whom you may acquire this knowledge." It seems that what is intended here is that, indeed, the scholars are the heirs of the prophets, but one must be careful in the choice of a person from whom to acquire the knowledge the prophets have bequeathed. It will contradict the obvious meaning of the tradition, therefore, to maintain that the Imāms are intended by the expression "heirs of the prophets" and that it is from them that people must acquire knowledge. Anyone acquainted with the traditions that relate to the status of the Imāms (ʿa) and the rank accorded them by the Most Noble Messenger (s) will immediately realize that it is not the Imāms but the scholars of the community who are intended in this tradition. Similar qualities and epithets have been used for the scholars in numerous other traditions; e.g., "The scholars of my community are like the prophets preceding me," and "The scholars of my community are like the prophets of the Children of Israel."

To conclude, then, it is obvious that the ʿulamā—the scholars—are intended here.

There is a second objection that might be raised here, which calls for clarification. It might be said that the expression: "The scholars are the heirs of the prophets" cannot be used as a proof of our thesis—the governance of the faqīh—since the prophets (anbiyā) have only one dimension of prophethood, which is that they derive knowledge from an exalted source by means of revelation, inspiration, or some other method, and this does not imply or require rule over the people or the believers. If God Almighty has not bestowed leadership and rule on the prophets, they can in no wise possess it; they are only prophets in the narrow sense of the word. If they have been ordained to communicate the knowledge they have received, then it will be their duty at most to communicate it to the people. For in our traditions, a distinction is made between the prophet (nabī) and the messenger (rasūl): the latter has the mission of communicating the knowledge he has received, while the former merely receives it. In addition, the state of prophethood (nubuwwat) is different from that of governance (wilāyat), and it is this titular designation of "prophet" (nabī) that has been used in this tradition. The scholars have been made the successors of the prophets with respect to this titular designation, and since this designation does not imply or necessitate governance (wilāyat), we cannot deduce from the tradition that the scholars are to possess governance. If the Imām had said that the scholars hold the rank of Moses or Jesus, we would naturally infer that the scholars possess all of the aspects and qualities of Moses or Jesus, including governance, but since he did not say this and did not assign to the scholars the rank of any particular person among the prophets, we cannot draw that particular conclusion from the tradition in question.

In answer to this objection, it must first be stated that the criterion for the understanding of traditions and their wording must be common usage and current understanding, not precise technical analysis, and we, too, follow this criterion. Once a faqīh tries to introduce subtle technical points into the understanding of traditions, many matters become obscured. So, if we examine the expression: "The scholars are the heirs of the prophets" in the light of common usage, will it occur to us that only the titular designation of "prophet" is intended in the tradition, and that the scholars are heirs only to what is implied in that designation? Or on the contrary, does this expression provide a general principle that can be applied to individual prophets? To put it differently, if we were to ask someone who is aware only of the common usage of word, "Is such-and-such a faqīh a successor of Moses and Jesus?" He would answer—in the light of the tradition under discussion—"Yes, because Moses and Jesus are prophets." Again, if we were to ask, "Is the faqīh an heir to the Most Noble Messenger (s)?" he would answer, "Yes, because the Most Noble Messenger is one of the prophets."

We cannot, therefore, take the word "prophets" as a titular designation, particularly since it is in the plural. If the singular "prophet" were used in the tradition, then it might be possible that only the titular designation was intended, but since the plural is used, it means "every one of the prophets," not "every one of the prophets with respect to that by virtue of which they are prophets." This latter sense would indeed indicate that the titular designation exclusively was intended, as distinct from all other designations, so that the expression would come to mean, "The *faqīh* enjoys the stature of the prophet (*nabī*), but not that of the messenger (*rasūl*) nor that of the ruler (*walī*)." Analyses and interpretations like these, however, go against both common usage and reason.

For a third objection, let us suppose that the scholars are given the stature of the prophets with respect to their titular designation, with respect to that by virtue of which they are prophets. We must then regard the scholars as possessing all the attributes that God Almighty has designated the prophets as possessing, in accordance with this same equation of the scholars with the prophets. If, for example, some one says that so-and-so enjoys the same rank as the just and says next that we must honor the just, we infer from the two statements taken together that we must honor the person in question. This being the case, we can infer from the Qur'anic verse: "The prophet has higher claims on the believers than their own selves" (33:6) that the *'ulamā* possess the function of governance just as the prophet does. For what is implicit in having "higher claims" is precisely governance and command. In commenting upon the verse in question, the work *Majma' al-Bahrayn*[292] cites a tradition of Imām al-Bāqir ('a): "This verse was revealed concerning governance and command". The prophet, then, is empowered to rule and govern over the believers, and the same rule and governance that has been established for the Most Noble Messenger (s) is also established for the scholars for both in the verse quoted and in the tradition under discussion the titular designation "prophet" has been used.

We can, moreover, refer to a number of verses that designate the prophet as possessing various qualities and attributes, as, for example: "Obey God and obey the Messenger and the holders of authority from among you" (Qur'an, 4:59). Although a distinction is made in certain traditions between "prophet" and "messenger" with respect to the mode of revelation, rationally and in common usage the two words denote the same meaning. According to common usage, the "prophet" is one who receives tidings from God, and the "messenger" is one who conveys to mankind what he has received from God.

A fourth objection might also be raised. The ordinances that the Most Noble Messenger (s) left are a form of legacy, even though they are not designated technically as such, and those who take up those ordinances are his heirs. But what proof is there that the function of governance that the Prophet (s) exercised could be bequeathed and inherited? It might be that what could be bequeathed and inherited consisted only of his ordinances and his traditions, for the tradition states that the prophets bequeathed knowledge, or, in the version narrated by Abu 'l-Bukhturi, that they bequeathed "a legacy of their sayings and traditions." It is apparent, then, that they bequeathed their traditions, but governance cannot be bequeathed or inherited.

This objection is also unjustified. For governance and command are extrinsic and rational matters; concerning these matters, we must have recourse to rational persons. We might ask them whether they regard the transfer of governance and rule from one

---

[292] There are a number of works by this title. The reference here may be to the Qur'an commentary written in the eleventh/seventh century by Ziyā ad-Dīn Yūsuf Qazvīni. See Āqā Buzurg Tehrāni, *Adh-Dhāri'ah ilā Tasānif ash-Shī'ah* (Tehran, 1390/1970), XX, 23.

person to another by way of bequest as possible. For example, if a rational person is asked, "Who is heir to the rule in such-and-such a country?" will he answer that the position of ruler cannot be inherited, or say instead that such-and-such a person is the heir to the crown and the throne? "Heir the throne" is a well-known current expression. There can be no doubt that rationally speaking governance can be transferred from one person to another just like property that is inherited. If one considers first the verse: "The prophet has higher claims on the believers than their own selves," and then the tradition: "The scholars are the heirs of the prophets," he will realize that both refer to the same thing: extrinsic matters that are rationally capable of being transferred from one person to another.

If the phrase: "The scholars are the heirs of the prophets" referred to the Imāms ('a)—as does the tradition to the effect that the Imāms are the heirs of the Prophet (s) in all things—we would not hesitate to say that the Imāms are indeed the heirs of Prophet in all things, and no one could say that the legacy intended here refers only to knowledge and legal questions. So if we had before us only the sentence: "The scholars are the heirs of the prophets" and could disregard the beginning and end of the tradition, it would appear that all functions of the Most Noble Messenger ('a) that were capable of being transmitted—including rule over people—and that devolved on the Imāms after him, pertain also to the *fuqahā*, with the exception of those functions that must be excluded for other reasons and which we too exclude wherever there is reason to do so.

The major problem still remaining is that the sentence: "The scholars are heirs of the prophets" occurs in a context suggesting that the traditions of the prophets constitute their legacy. The authentic tradition narrated by Qaddāh reads: "The prophets bequeathed not a single dīnar or dirham; instead they bequeathed knowledge." That related by Abū 'l–Bukhtūri reads: "Although the prophets did not bequeath a single dīnar or dirham; they bequeathed their sayings and traditions." These statements provide a context suggesting that the legacy of the prophets is their traditions, and that nothing else has survived of them that might be inherited, particularly since the particle "*innamā*" occurs in the text of the tradition, indicating exclusivity.

But even this objection is faulty. For if the meaning were indeed that the Most Noble Messenger (s) had left nothing of himself that might be inherited except his traditions, this would contradict the very bases of our Shi'ah school. The Prophet (s) did indeed leave things that could be inherited, and there is no doubt that among them was his exercise of rule over the community, which was transmitted by him to the Commander of the Faithful ('a), and then to each of the other Imāms ('a) in succession. The particle "*innamā*" does not always indicate exclusivity, and indeed there are doubts that it ever does; in addition, "*innamā*" does not occur in the text narrated by Qaddāh but only in that related by Abu 'l- Bukhturi whose chain of transmission is weak, as I have already said.

Now let us examine in turn each of the sentences in the text narrated by Qaddāh in order to see whether the context does, in fact, indicate that the legacy of the prophets consists exclusively of their traditions.

"For whoever travels a path in search of knowledge, God opens up a path to paradise." This is a sentence in praise of scholars, but not in praise of *any* scholar, so that we imagine the sentence to be uniformly praising all types of scholar. Look up the traditions in *al-Kāfi* concerning the attributes and duties of scholars, and you will see that in order to become a scholar and an heir of the prophets, it is not enough to study a few lines. The scholar also has duties he must perform, and therein lies the real difficulty of his calling.

"The angels lower their wings before him as a sign of their being well pleased with him." The meaning of "lower their wings" is obvious to those who concern themselves with these matters. It is an act signifying humility and respect.

"All that is in the heavens and on earth, even the fish in the ocean, seeks forgiveness for him." This sentence does not require detailed explanation because it is not relevant to our present theme.

"The superiority of the learned man over the mere worshipper is like that of the full moon over the stars." The meaning of this sentence is clear.

"Truly the scholars are the heirs of the prophets." The entire tradition, from its beginning down to and including this sentence, is in praise of the scholars and in exposition of their virtues and qualities, one of these qualities being that they are the heirs of the prophets. Being the heirs of the prophets becomes a virtue for the scholars when they exercise governance and rule over people, like the prophets, and obedience to them is a duty.

The meaning of the next expression in the tradition, "The prophets bequeathed not a single dinār or dirham," is not that they bequeathed nothing but learning and traditions. Rather it is an indication that although the prophets exercised authority and ruler over people, they were men of God, not materialistic creatures trying to accumulate worldly wealth. It also implies that the form of government exercised by the prophets was different from monarchies and other current forms of government, which have served as means for the enrichment and gratification of the rulers.

The way of life of the Most Noble Messenger (s) was extremely simple. He did not use his authority and position to enrich his material life in the hope of leaving a legacy. What he did leave behind was knowledge, the most noble of all things, and in particular, knowledge derived from God Almighty. Indeed, the singling out of knowledge for mention in this tradition may have been precisely because of its nobility.

It cannot be said that since the qualities of the scholars are mentioned in this verse together with their being heirs to knowledge and not heirs to property, therefore, the scholars are heirs *only* to knowledge and traditions.

In certain cases, the phrase: "What we leave behind is charity" has been added to the tradition, but it does not truly belong there. Found only in Sunni versions of the traditions, it has been added for political reasons.[293]

The most we can say with respect to the context these sentences provide for the statement: "The scholars are heirs to the prophets" is that the statement cannot be taken in an absolute sense, which would mean that everything that pertains to the prophets also pertains to the scholars. Nor can the statement, because of its context, be taken in the restricted sense that the scholars are heirs *only* to the knowledge of the prophets. If that were sense, the tradition would contradict the other traditions we

---

[293] After the death of the Prophet (s), his daughter Fātimah asked for the arable lands near Fadak (a small town near Medina) to be assigned to her as a legacy from her father, since in his lifetime the Prophet had used the produce of the land for the upkeep of his wives. Abū Bakr refused, citing the alleged words of the Prophet: "We prophets bequeath no legacies; what we leave behind is charity (*sadaqah*)." See al-Balādhūri, *al-Futūh*, ed. de Goeje (Leiden, Netherlands, 1886), pp. 29-33. For Shī'i tradition, Fadak became a symbol of unjust denial. "The Shī'ah traditionists and exegetes and some Sunni scholars write: "When the verse: *Give the kinsmen his due, and the needy, and the wayfarer*...(Sūrah Isrā, 17:26) was revealed the Prophet called her daughter Fātimah and made over Fadak to her" [Majma' al-Bayān, vol. III, p. 411; Sharh-i Ibn Abi 'l-Hadīd, vol. XVI, p. 248]. And the narrator of this incident is Abū Sa'īd al-Khudri who was one of the distinguished companions of the Prophet." Subhāni, *The Message*, chap. 44, "The Story of Fadak,"

quoted earlier in connection with our theme and tend to neglect them. This restricted sense cannot be derived from this.

For the sake of argument, if it were true that this tradition means that the Most Noble Messenger (s), left no legacy but knowledge, and that rulership and governance can be neither bequeathed nor inherited, and if, too, we did not infer from the Prophet's saying: "'Ali is my heir" that the Commander of the Faithful ('a) was indeed his successor, then we would be obliged to have recourse to *nass*[294] with respect to the successorship of the Commander of the Faithful and the remaining Imāms ('a). We would then follow the same method with respect to the exercise of governance by the *faqīh*, for according to the tradition cited above, the *fuqahā* have been appointed to the function of successorship and rule. Thus, we have reconciled this tradition with those that indicate appointment.

In his *'Awā'id*,[295] Narāqi quotes the following tradition from the *Fiqh-i Razāvi*:[296] "The rank of the *faqīh* in the present age is like that of the prophets of the Children of Israel." Naturally, we cannot claim that the *Fiqh-i Razāvi* was actually composed by Imām Ridā ('a), but it is permissible to quote it as a further support for our thesis.

It must be understood that what is meant by "the prophets of the Children of Israel" is indeed the prophets, not *fuqahā* who lived in the time of Moses and may have been called prophets for some reason or other. The *fuqahā* who lived in the time of Moses were all subject to his authority, and exercised their functions in obedience to him. It may be that when he dispatched them somewhere to convey a message, he would also appoint them as "holder of authority"—naturally, we are not precisely informed about these matters—but it is obvious that Moses himself was one of the prophets of the Children of Israel, and that all of the functions that existed for the Most Noble Messenger (s) also existed for Moses, with a difference, of course, in rank, station, and degree. We deduce from the general scope of the word "rank" in this tradition, therefore, that the same function of rulership and governance that Moses exercised exists also for *fuqahā*.

The *Jāmi' al-Akhbār*[297] contains the following tradition of the Most Noble Messenger (s): "On the Day of Judgment I will take pride in the scholars of my community, for the scholars of my community are like the prophets preceding me." This tradition also serves to support my thesis.

In the *Mustadrak*,[298] a tradition is quoted from the *Ghurār*[299] to the following effect: "The scholars are rulers over the people." One version reads "*hukamā*" ("wise men") instead of "*hukkām*" ("rulers"), but this appears to be incorrect. According to the *Ghurār*, the form "*hukkām*" is correct. The meaning of this tradition is self-evident, and if its chain of transmission is valid, it may also serve to support my thesis.

---

[294] *Nass*: a clear and authoritative text, unequivocal in its meaning.

[295] Narāqi (n. 107 above) wrote a comprehensive book on the principles of *fiqh* entitled *'Awā'id al-Ayyām min Qawā'id al-Fuqahā al-A'lam*.

[296] *Fiqh-i Razāvi*: a work purporting to contain the legal pronouncements of Imām Ridā, of disputed authenticity. See Tehrāni, *adh-Dhāri'ah*, XVI, 292-293.

[297] See n. 74 above.

[298] *Mustadrak*: that is, *Mustadrak al-Wasā'il*, a supplement to *Wasā'il ash-Shī'ah* (see n. 105) composed by Mīrzā Husayn Nūri (d. 1320/1902).

[299] Possibly *Ghurār al-Farā'id was Durar al-Qalā'id*, a work on the principles of *fiqh* by Muhsīn ibn Hasan al-A'raji (d.1227/1812). See Tehrāni, *Adh-Dhāri'ah*, XVI, 41-42.

There are still additional traditions that may be quoted. One of them is quoted in *Tuhāf al-'Uqūl*[300] under the heading: "The Conduct of Affairs and the Enforcement of Ordinances by the Scholars." This tradition consists of two parts. The first is a tradition transmitted by the Doyen of the Martyrs ('a) from the Commander of the Faithful, 'Ali ('a), and concerns the enjoining of the good and the prohibition of the evil. The second part is the speech of the Doyen of the Martyrs concerning the governance of the *faqīh* and the duties that are incumbent upon the *fuqahā*, such as the struggle against oppressors and tyrannical governments in order to establish an Islamic government and implement the ordinances of Islam. In the course of this celebrated speech, which he delivered at Mīnah,[301] he set forth the reasons for his own *jihād* against the tyrannical Umayyad state. Two important themes may be deduced from this tradition. The first is the principle of the governance of the *faqīh*, and the second is that the *fuqahā*, by means of *jihād* and enjoying the good and forbidding the evil, must expose and overthrow tyrannical rulers and rouse the people so that the universal movement of all alert Muslims can establish Islamic government in place of tyrannical regimes.

This is the tradition.[302] The Doyen of the Martyrs ('a) said: "O people, take heed of the counsel God gave His friends when he rebuked the rabbis by saying, 'Why do their scholars and rabbis not forbid their sinful talk and consumption of what is forbidden [that is, such talk and consumption on the part of the Jews]? Truly what they have done is evil' (Qur'an, 5:63). Again God says: "Cursed by the tongue of David and Jesus, son of Mary, are those among the Children of Israel who have failed to believe on account of their rebellion and transgression. They did not prevent each other from committing vile and corrupt acts; truly what they did was abominable!" (Qur'an, 5:78). God blamed and reproached them because they saw with their own eyes the oppressors committing vile and corrupt acts but did not stop them, out of love for the income they received from them as well as fear of persecution and injury. However, God orders us to fear Him, not men, and He says: "And the believing men and women are friends and protectors of each other; they enjoin the good and forbid the evil" (Qur'an, 9:71).

"We see that this verse, in the course of enumerating the attributes of the believers, the attributes that indicate mutual affection, solitude, and desire to guide each other, God begins with enjoining the good and forbidding the evil, considering this the prime duty. For He knows that if this duty is performed and is established within society, performance of all other duties will follow, from the easiest to the most difficult. The reason for this is that enjoining the good and forbidding the evil means summoning people to Islam, which is a struggle to establish correct belief in the face of external opposition, while at the same time vindicating the rights of the oppressed; opposing and struggling against oppressors within the community; and endeavoring to ensure that public wealth and the income derived from war are distributed in accordance with the just laws of Islam, and that taxes [*zakāt* and all other forms of fiscal income, whether compulsory or voluntary] are collected, levied, and expended in due and proper form.

---

[300] *Tuhāf al-'Uqūl*: a collection of sermons and aphorisms of the Imāms compiled by Shaykh Muhammad al-Halabi, a contemporary of Shaykh Sadūq and teacher of Shaykh Mufīd.

[301] Mīnah: a small town near Mecca.

[302] Imām Khomeini quotes the Arabic text of the tradition before giving his own translation in Persian. We have rendered into English only the Persian translation, which is slightly fuller in parts than the Arabic original.

"O scholars, you who are celebrated and enjoy good repute on account of your learning! You have achieved fame in society because of your devotion, the good counsel you impart, and the guidance you dispense. It is on account of God that men venerate and stand in awe of you, so that even the powerful fear you and feel compelled to rise respectfully before you, and men who are not subject to you and over whom you hold no authority willingly regard themselves as your subordinates and grant you favors they deny themselves. When the people do not receive their due from the public treasury, you intervene and act with the awesomeness and imperiousness of monarchs and the stature of the great. Have you not earned all these forms of respect and prestige because of men's hopes that you will implement God's laws, even though in most instances you have failed to do so?

"You have failed to enforce most of the rights you were entrusted to preserve. For instance, you have neglected the rights of the oppressed and the lowly, squandered the rights of the weak and the powerless, but pursed assiduously what you regard as your personal rights. You have not spent your money or risked your lives for the sake of the One Who gave you life, nor have you fought against any group or tribe for the sake of God. You desire, and regard it as your due, that He should grant you paradise, the company of the Prophet, and security from hellfire in the hereafter. You who have such expectations of God, I fear that the full weight of His wrath will descend upon you, for although it is by his might and glory that you have achieved high rank, you show no respect to those who truly know God and wish to disseminate their knowledge while you yourselves enjoy respect among God's bondsmen on His account.

"I am also afraid for you for another reason: you see the covenants enacted with God[*] being violated and trampled underfoot; yet you show no anxiety. When it comes to the covenants enacted with your fathers, you become greatly disturbed and anxious if they are only violated in part, but the pledges you have given to the Most Noble Messenger[**] are a matter of complete indifference to you. The blind, the dumb, and the poverty-stricken cultivators of the land everywhere lack protectors and no mercy is shown them. You do not behave in accordance with your function and rank, nor do you support or pay any regard to those who do so behave and who strive to promote the standing of the religious scholars. You purchase your safety from the oppressive ruling powers with flattery, cajolery and compromise.

"All these activities have been forbidden you by God, and He has, moreover, commanded you to forbid each other to engage in them, but you pay no attention. The disaster that has befallen you is greater than what has befallen others, for the true rank and degree of 'ulamā has been taken away from you. The administration of the country, the issuing of judicial decrees, and the approving of legislative programs should actually be entrusted to religious scholars who are guardians of the rights of God and knowledgeable about God's ordinances concerning what is permitted and what is forbidden. But your position has been usurped from you, for no other reason than that you have abandoned the pivot of truth—the law of Islam and God's decree—and have disagreed about the nature of the Sunnah, despite the existence of clear proofs.

---

[*] That is, the social contracts that establish the institutions of society and determine social relations in Islam. (Kh.)

[**] That is, Islamic relationships based upon the oath of loyalty sworn to the Prophet and similar pledge to obey and follow his successors, 'Ali and his descendants, given to the Prophet at the pool of Khum. (Kh).

"If you were true men, strong in the face of torture and suffering and prepared to endure hardship for God's sake, then all proposed regulations would be brought to you for your approval and for you to issue; authority would lie in your hands. But you allowed the oppressors to take away your function, and permitted that the government, which is supposed to be regulated by the provisions of the *sharī'ah*, to fall into their hands so that they administer it on the shaky basis of their own conjectures and suppositions and make arbitrariness and the satisfaction of lust their consistent practice. What enabled them to gain control of government was your fleeing in panic from being killed, your attachment to the transitory life of this world. With that mentality and the conduct it inspires, you have delivered the powerless masses into the clutches of the oppressors. While some cringe like slaves under the blows of the oppressors, and others search in misery and desperation for bread and water, the rulers are entirely absorbed in the pleasures of kingship, earning shame and disgrace for themselves with their licentiousness, following evil counselors, and showing impudence toward God. One of their appointed spokesmen mounts the *minbar*[303] in each city. The soil of the homeland is defenseless before them, and they grab freely whatever they want of it. The people are their slaves, and are powerless to defend themselves. One ruler is a dictator by nature, malevolent and rancorous; another represses his wretched subjects ruthlessly, plundering by imposing on them all kinds of burdens; and still another refuses in his absolutism to recognize either God or the Day of Judgment! Is it not strange—how can one not think it strange—that society is in the clutches of a cunning oppressor whose tax collectors are oppressors and whose governors feel no compassion or mercy toward the believers under their rule?

"It is God Who will judge concerning what is at dispute among us and deliver a decisive verdict concerning all that occurs among us.

"O God! You know that everything we did [that is, the struggle in which they had recently engaged against the Umayyads] was not prompted by rivalry for political power, nor by a search for wealth and abundance; rather it was done in order to demonstrate to men the shining principles and values of Your religion, to reform the affairs of Your land, to protect and secure the indisputable rights of Your oppressed servants, and to act in accordance with the duties You have established and the norms, laws, and ordinances You have decreed.

"So, O scholars of religion! You are to help us reach this goal, win back our rights from those powers who have considered it acceptable to wrong you and who have attempted to put out the light kindled by your Prophet. God the One suffices us—upon Him do we rely, to Him do we turn, in His hands lies our fate, and to Him shall we return."

When the Doyen of the Martyrs ('a) said at the beginning of this sermon: "O people, take heed of the counsel God gave His friends when He rebuked the rabbis," his address was not restricted to a particular group of people—those present in the assembly, the inhabitants of a certain city, town, or country, or even all people alive in the world at the time. Rather it embraces all who hear the summons at whatever time, for it begins with the expression "O people" (*yā ayyuha 'n-nās*), which occurs in the Qur'an with the same universal meaning.[304] When God rebukes the rabbis—the Jewish scholars—and condemns their behavior, He is at the same time addressing His friends (*awliyā*) and advising them. The word "*awliyā*" means here those who have

---

[303] *Minbar*: the pulpit in the mosque.
[304] See, for example, 2:168, 4:170, 7:150, 10:57, and many other verses.

set their faces toward God and hold responsible positions in society, not the Twelve Imāms.[305]

God says in the verse we are examining: "Why do their scholars and rabbis not forbid their sinful talk and consumption of what is forbidden? Truly what they have done is evil." Thus He reproaches the rabbit and Jewish religious scholars for failing to prevent the oppressors' sinful talk—a term that includes lying, slander, distorting the truth, and so forth—and consumption of what is forbidden. It is obvious that, this reproach and upbraiding is not confined to the scholars of the Jews, nor for that matter to those of the Christians; it applies also to the religious scholars in Islamic society, or indeed, any other society. If the religious scholars of Islamic society are silent, therefore, in the face of the policies of the oppressors, they too are reproached and condemned by God; and here there is no distinction between scholars of the past, present, and future—they are equal in this regard. The Doyen of the Martyrs ('a) made reference to this verse of Qur'an so that the religious scholars of Islamic society would take heed, awaken, and no longer neglect their duty of enjoining the good and forbidding the evil or stay silent in the face of the oppressive and deviant ruling classes.

There are two points to which he draws attention by citing this verse. First, the religious scholars' neglect of their duties is more harmful than the failure of others to perform their normal duties. If a bazaar merchant, for example, does something wrong, it is only he who suffers the harm that results. But if the religious scholars fail in fulfilling their duties, by keeping silent, let us say, in the face of tyranny, Islam itself suffers as a result. But if, on the contrary, they act in accordance with their duty and speak out when they should, eschewing silence, then Islam itself will benefit.

Secondly, although all things contrary to the *sharī'ah* must be forbidden, emphasis has been placed on sinful talk and consumption of what is forbidden, implying that these two evils are more dangerous than all the others and must therefore be more diligently combated. Sometimes the statements and propaganda put forth by oppressive regimes are more harmful to Islam and the Muslims than their actions and policy, endangering the whole repute of Islam and the Muslims. God reproaches the religious scholars, therefore, for failing to prevent the oppressors from uttering dishonest words and spreading sinful propaganda. He says in effect: "Why did they not denounce the man who falsely claimed to be God's vicegerent on earth and the instrument of His will, who claimed to be enforcing God's laws in the right way and to have a correct understanding and practice of Islamic justice, even though he was incapable of comprehending what justice is? Claims like these are a form of sinful talk that is extremely harmful to society. Why did the religious scholars not prevent them from being made? The tyrants who uttered this nonsense talk and committed treason and brought evil innovations[306] into Islam; why did the religious scholars not stand in their way and make them desist from these sins?

If someone interprets God's ordinances in a way displeasing to Him, thus introducing an evil innovation in Islam, or executes laws that are anti-Islamic, claiming to be acting in accordance with the requirements of Islamic justice, it is the duty of the religious scholars to proclaim their opposition. If they fail to do so, they will be cursed by God, as is apparent both from the verse under discussion and from this tradition:

---

[305] The word *awliyā*—like the cognate *wilāyat*—has numerous different meanings. It is used here in the general sense that can be deduced from Qur'an, 10:62-63: "Verily the friends (*awliyā*) of God—those who believe and guard against evil—shall suffer no fear nor shall they grieve."

[306] Evil innovation: *bid'at*, a belief or practice not compatible with either the Qur'an or the Sunnah.

"When evil innovations appear, it is the duty of the scholars to bring forth his knowledge [by condemning them]; otherwise, God's curse will be upon him."

In such cases, the expression of opposition and the expounding of God's teachings and ordinances that stand in contradiction to innovation, oppression, and sin, are also useful in themselves, for they make the masses aware of the corruption of society and the wrongdoing of the treacherous, sinful, and irreligious rulers. The people will then rise up in revolt and refuse to collaborate any longer with the tyrants or to obey corrupt and treacherous ruling powers. The expression of opposition by religious scholars is a form of "forbidding the evil" on the part of the religious leadership, which creates in its wake a wave of broad opposition and "forbidding the evil" on the part of all religiously inclined and honorable people. If the oppressive and deviant rulers do not bow to the wishes of such an oppositional movement by returning to the straight path of Islam and obedience to God's laws, but attempt to silence it by force of arms, they will, in effect, have engaged in armed aggression against the Muslims and acquired the status of a rebellious group (*fi'a bāghiya*). It will then be the duty of the Muslims to engage in an armed *jihād* against that ruling group in order to make the policies of the ruling society and the norms of government conform to the principles and ordinances of Islam.

It is true that at present, you do not have the power to prevent the innovative practices of the rulers or to halt the corruption in which they are engaged. But at least do not stay silent. If they strike you on head, cry out in protest! Do not submit to oppression; such submission is worse than oppression itself. In order to counteract their press and propaganda apparatus, we must create our own apparatus to refuse whatever lies they issue and to proclaim that Islamic justice is not what they claim it is, but on the contrary, has a complete and coherent program for ordering the affairs of the family and all Muslim society. All these matters must be made clear so that people can come to know the truth and coming generations will not take the silence of the religious leaders as proof that the deeds and policies of the oppressors conform to the *sharī'ah*, and that the perspicacious religion of Islam allows them to "consume what is forbidden," or in other words, to plunder the wealth of the people.

Since the range of thought of some people is confined to the mosque we are now sitting in and is incapable of extending any further, when they hear the expression "consumption of what is forbidden," they can only think of some corner grocer whose is (God forbid) selling his customers short. They never think of the whole range of more important forms of "consuming what is forbidden," of plunder. Huge amounts of capital are being swallowed up; our public funds are being embezzled; our oil is being plundered; and our country is turned into a market for expensive, unnecessary goods by the representatives of foreign companies, which makes it possible for foreign capitalists and their local agents to pocket the people's money. A number of foreign states carry off our oil after drawing it out of the ground, and the negligible sum they pay to the regime they have installed returns to their pockets by other routes. As for the small amount that goes into the treasury, God only knows what it is spent on. All of this is a form of "consumption of what is forbidden" that takes place on an enormous scale, in fact on an international scale. It is not merely an evil, but a hideous and most dangerous evil. Examine carefully the conditions of society and the actions of the government and its component organs, and then you will understand what hideous "consumption of what is forbidden" is taking place now. If an earthquake occurs in some corners of the country, it too becomes a means for the ruling profiteers to increase their illegal income: they fill their pockets with money that is supposed to go to the victims of the earthquake. Whenever our oppressive, anti-national rulers

70

enter into agreements with foreign states or companies, they pocket huge amounts of our people's money and lavish additional huge sums on their foreign masters. It is a veritable flood of forbidden consumption that sweeps past us, right before our eyes. All this is misappropriation of wealth goes on and on: in our foreign trade and in the contracts made for the exploitation of our mineral wealth, the utilization of our forests and other natural resources, construction work, road building, and the purchase of arms from the imperialists, both Western and communist.

We must end all this plundering and usurpation of wealth. The people as a whole have a responsibility in this respect, but the responsibility of the religious scholars is graver and more critical. We must take the lead over other Muslims in embarking on this sacred *jihād*, this heavy undertaking; because of our rank and position, we must be in the forefront. If we do not have the power today to prevent these misdeeds from happening and to punish these embezzlers and traitors, these powerful thieves that rule over us, then we must work to gain that power. At the same time, to fulfill our minimum obligation, we must not fail to expound the truth and expose the thievery and mendacity of our rulers. When we come to power, we will not only put the country's political life, economy, and administration in order, we will also whip and chastise the thieves and the liars.

They set fire to the Masjid al-Aqsā.[307] We cry out: "Leave the Masjid al-Aqsā half-burned to the ground; do not erase all traces of the crime!" But the Shāh's regime opens an account, sets up a fund, and starts collecting money from the people supposedly to rebuilt the Masjid al-Aqsā, but really to fill the pockets of our rulers while also covering up the crime committed by Israel.

These are the disasters that are afflicting the nation of Islam, and that have brought us to our present state. Is it not duty of the scholars of Islam to speak out about all this? "Why do their rabbis not forbid their consumption of what is forbidden"? why do our Muslims scholars not protect? Why do they say nothing about all this plundering?

To return to the sermon of the Doyen of the Martyrs ('a), he continues with a reference to the verse: "Cursed are those among Children of Israel who have failed to believe" (5:78). This is not relevant to our present discussion. Then he says: "God reproached and blamed them [the rabbis] because they saw with their own eyes the oppressors committing vile and corrupt acts but did not stop them." According to the Doyen of the Martyrs, their silence was due to two factors: greed and baseness. Either they were covetous persons who profited materially from the oppressors, accepting payment to keep quiet, or they were faint-hearted cowards who were afraid of them.

Consult the traditions referring to enjoining the good and forbidding the evil. There the conduct of those who constantly invent excuses in order to escape from doing their duty is condemned and their silence is considered shameful. "God says: 'Do not fear men, but fear Me' (2:150). This verse means roughly: 'Why do you fear men? Our friends (*awliyā*) have given up their lives for the sake of Islam; you should be prepared to do the same.'

"Elsewhere in the Qur'an God also says: "The believers, men and women, are friends and protectors to each other; they enjoin the good and forbid the evil;...they establish the prayer, pay the *zakāt*, and obey God and His Messenger' (9:71). In this verse, God mentions the duty of enjoining the good and forbidding the evil first because He knows that if this duty is correctly performed, all other duties, whether easy or difficult, will fall into place. For enjoining the good and forbidding the evil means summoning men to Islam while at the same time remedying oppression, opposing the

---

[307] Masjid al-Aqsā: see n. 37 above.

oppressor, making just distribution of the spoils of war, and levying and spending taxes in just and due form."

If the duty of enjoining the good and forbidding the evil is properly performed, all other duties will automatically fall into place. If the good is enjoined and the evil forbidden, the oppressors and their agents will be unable to usurp the people's property and dispose of it according to their own whims; they will be unable to squander the taxes taken from the people. For he who enjoins the good and forbids the evil actively calls men to Islam by remedying injustice and opposing the oppressor.

Enjoining the good and forbidding the evil has been made a duty primarily for the sake of accomplishing these high aims. We have restricted it, however, to a narrow category of affairs where harm is suffered chiefly by the individual who is guilty of a sin by deed or by omission. We have the idea firmly in our heads that the instances of evil we are called upon to combat (*munkarāt*) are only the things we encounter or hear about in everyday life. For example, if someone plays music while we are riding on the bus,[308] or the owner of a coffee house does something wrong, or someone eats in the middle of the bazaar during Ramadān,[309] we regard all these things as instances of evil we must denounce. Meanwhile, we remain totally oblivious to far greater evils. Those who are destroying the welfare of Islam and trampling on the rights of the weak---it is they whom we must force to desist from evil.

If a collective protest were made against the oppressors who commit an improper act or crime, if several thousand telegrams were sent to them from all the Islamic countries telling them to desist, to relinquish their errors, they certainly would desist. If every time a step were taken or a speech given against the interests of Islam and the welfare of the people, those responsible were condemned throughout the country, in every single village and hamlet, they would be obliged to retreat. Could they possibly do otherwise? Never! I know them; I know what kind of people they are. They are very cowardly and would retreat very quickly. But if they see that we are more gutless than they are, they will give themselves airs and do whatever they want.

When the *'ulamā* of Qum met and banded together on one occasion, and the provinces supported them by sending delegations and delivering speeches to show their solidarity, the regime retreated and canceled the measures we were objecting to.[310] Afterwards, they were able to cool our enthusiasm and weaken us; they divided us up and invented a separate "religious duty" for each of us. As a result of the differing opinions that appeared among us, they grew bold again, and now they do whatever they want with the Muslims and this Islamic country of ours.

The Doyen of the Martyrs ('a) speaks of "summoning men to Islam while at the same time remedying oppression and opposing the oppressors"; it is for the sake of these great aims that enjoining the good and forbidding the evil has been made a duty. If some poor grocer does something wrong, he has not harmed Islam, but only himself.

---

[308] Among the different schools of Islamic law, the Shī'i School manifests the greatest disapproval of music. Music in a public place is doubly reprehensible since it is an imposition on the unwilling listener.

[309] There are certain circumstances that may dispense one from fasting during Ramadān, notably illness, but out of respect for the sanctity of the month and the fasting of others, one must refrain from eating in public.

[310] A reference to the agitation against the new laws on the election of local councils promulgated by the Shāh's regime on October 6, 1962. These laws no longer specified that candidates were to be Muslim, and they were seen as a prelude to increased participation in public life by the Bahā'is and eventual abolition of the Constitution of 1906. After a prolonged campaign against the laws, in which Imām Khomeini took a prominent part, they were annulled by the government on November 28, 1962. See S.H.R., *Barrasī va Tahlīlī*, pp. 142-187.

In performing our duty of enjoining the good and forbidding the evil, we must pay closest attention to those who harm Islam and those who, under various pretexts, plunder the people's means of livelihood.

On occasion we read in the paper—sometimes it is stated humorously, sometimes seriously—that many of the items collected for the victims of floods or earthquakes are picked up by our rulers for their own use. One of the *'ulamā* of Malāyer told me that the people had wanted to send a truckload of shrouds for the victims of some disaster, but the police refused to let them through, and even tried to confiscate the load! "Enjoining the good and forbidding the evil" is more imperative in such cases.

Now let me ask you, were the subjects mentioned by the Doyen of the Martyrs ('a) in his sermon addressed only to his companions who were gathered around him listening to his words? Does not the phrase "O people, take heed" address us too? Are we not included in "people"? Should we not profit from this address of the Doyen of the Martyrs ('a)?

As I stated at the beginning of this discussion, the subjects contained in the sermon of the Doyen of the Martyrs ('a) were not intended for a single group or class. His address was more in the nature of a circular directed to all commanders, ministers, rulers, *fuqahā*—and in short, to the whole world, particularly those who are alive and fully conscious. The circulars he issued belong together with the Qur'an in the sense that they demand our obedience until the Day of Resurrection. The verse referred to in the address speaks only of the Jewish scholars and rabbis, but its purport is universal. The Jewish scholars and rabbis were condemned by God because fear or covetousness made them keep silent in the face of the misdeeds of the oppressors, whereas if they had spoken or cried out in protest, they could have prevented oppression from occurring. If the *'ulamā* of Islam likewise fail to rise up against the oppressors and remain silent instead, they too will be condemned.

After addressing the people in general, the Doyen of the Martyrs ('a) then turns to a particular group, the *'ulamā* of Islam, and tells them: "You enjoy prestige and standing in society; the nation of Islam respects and venerates you. You are held in awe and have high standing in society because you are expected to rise up against the oppressors in defense of the truth and to compel the oppressor to enforce the rights of the oppressed. Men have placed their hopes in you for the establishment of justice and the prevention of transgression by the oppressors.

"Thus you have reached a certain station and rank. But you have failed to perform the duties of your station. If some harm were to befall the father of one of you, or if—God forbid—someone were to insult him, you would be greatly distressed and would cry out in protest. But now that God's covenants are being violated before your very eyes and Islam is being dishonored, you keep silent and are not distressed even in your hearts for if you were distressed, you would be bound to raise your voices in protest. The blind, the dumb, and the poverty-stricken cultivators of the land are being destroyed and nobody shows any concern; no one is concerned for the wretched, barefooted people."

Do you imagine all that bombastic propaganda being broadcast on the radio is true? Go and see for yourselves at first hand what state our people are living in. Not even one, out of two hundred villages has a clinic. No one is concerned about the poor and the hungry, and they do not allow the measures Islam has devised for the sake of the poor to be implemented. Islam has solved the problem of poverty and inscribed it at the very top of its program: "*Sadaqāt* is for the poor."[311] Islam is aware that first, the

---

[311] Qur'an, 9:60.

conditions of the poor must be remedied; the conditions of the deprived must be remedied. But *they* do not allow the plans of Islam to be implemented.

Our wretched people subsist in conditions of poverty and hunger, while the taxes that the ruling class extorts from them are squandered. They buy Phantom jets so that pilots from Israel and its agents can come and train in them in our country.[312] So extensive is the influence of Israel in our country—Israel, which is in a state of war with the Muslims, so that those who support it are likewise in a state of war with the Muslims—and so great is the support the regime gives it, that Israeli soldiers come to our country for training! Our country has become a base for them! The markets of our country are also in their hands. If matters go on this way, and the Muslims continue to be apathetic, the Muslims will lose all say in the commercial life of the country.

To return to the address of the Doyen of the Martyrs ('a): "You have not made proper use of your station. Not only you do nothing yourselves; you fail to support the person who does want to do his duty. The only source of concern and satisfaction for you is that you have the support and respect of the oppressor, that he addresses you as 'Noble Shaykh'! What the nation suffers at the hands of the government is of no concern to you. The disaster that has befallen you is greater than what has befallen others for the true rank and degree of 'ulamā has been taken away from you. The administration of affairs and the implementation of law ought to be undertaken by those who are knowledgeable concerning God and are trustees of God's ordinances concerning what is permitted and what is forbidden. But that rank has been taken away from you."

The Imām ('a) could have said at this point: "What is my right has been taken away from me, but you have not come to my aid," or, "The rights of Imāms have been taken away, but you have kept silent." Instead, he spoke of those "knowledgeable concerning God" (*al-'ulamā bi-'llāh*), meaning the religious scholars (*rabbāniyūn*) or leaders. Here he is not referring to the philosophers or mystics, for the person knowledgeable concerning God is the one who is learned in God's ordinances. It is such a person who is designated as a religious scholar (*rūhāni* or *rabbāni*), naturally on condition that spirituality (*rūhāniyyat*) and orientation to God Almighty be fully apparent in him

The Imām went on: "But your position has been usurped from you, for no other reason but that you have abandoned the pivot of truth and have disagreed about the nature of the Sunnah, despite the existence of clear proofs. But if you were to show strength in the face of hardship and suffering for God's sake, then the conduct of affairs, as willed by God, would be restored to you; command and authority would be yours."

If you were to act correctly and perform your duty, you would see that the conduct of affairs would be bound over to you. If the form of government willed by Islam were to come into being, none of the governments now existing in the world would be able to resist it; they would all capitulate. But unfortunately, we have failed to establish such a government. Even in the earliest age of Islam, its opponents hindered its establishment and prevented governments from being entrusted to the person chosen by God and His Messenger precisely in order to prevent what has happened.

---

[312] One indication of the close ties existing with Israel was the regular contacts that took place between Iranian generals and high-ranking members of the Zionist armed forces. For example, General Palizban met in Occupied Palestine with Moshe Dayan and Arik Sharon, most probably in 1974. Photographs of the meeting, showing all participants with cordial smiles, were discovered after the Revolution and published in the newspaper *Jumhūrī-yi Islāmī* on Shahrīvar 26, 1359/September 17, 1980.

"You allowed the oppressors to take away your functions." When you failed to perform your duties and abandoned the task of government, it became possible for the oppressors to take over the position that was legitimately yours. "You allowed the affairs of God to fall into their hands, so they came to conduct them on the basis of their suppositions and arbitrary desires. What enabled them to win this control was your panic-stricken flight from being killed, and your attachment to the life of this world. You have delivered the powerless into their clutches, so that some of the people are now subjugated like slaves and others are deprived of even their livelihood." All of this applies to the age we live in; in fact, it applies more fully to the present than to the time of the Imām ('a). "The rulers are entirely absorbed in the pleasures of kingship, earning shame and disgrace for themselves with their licentiousness, following evil counselors, and showing impudence toward God. One of their appointed spokesmen mounts the   minbar in each city to tell lies." In those days preachers would praise the oppressors from the minbar. Today, radio stations fill the air with propaganda on their behalf and maliciously misrepresent the ordinances of Islam.

"The earth is defenseless against them." Now, too, the oppressors can freely exploit the earth, without any obstruction; there is no one to stand in their way. "They grab freely whatever they want [of the earth]. The people are their slaves and are powerless to defend themselves. One ruler is an obstinate tyrant, while another represses his wretched subjects ruthlessly, and still another refuses in his absolutism to recognize God as the beginning and end of all things. Is it not strange—how could one not think it strange—that the world is in the clutches of cunning tyrants, oppressive tax collectors, and governors who have no compassion for the believers under their rule?

"It is God Who will judge concerning what is at dispute among us, and deliver a decisive verdict concerning all that occurs among us.

"O God! You know that everything we did was not prompted by rivalry for political power, nor by desire for the chattels of this world. Rather, it was done in order to demonstrate the signs of Your religion, to reform the affairs of your land, to protect the oppressed among Your servants, and to act in accordance with the duties, norms, and ordinances You have established.

"So, O scholars of religion! Help us reach our goal and obtain our rights. The oppressors will wax strong in their efforts against you and will attempt to put out the light kindled by your Beloved [the Prophet]. But God suffices us; upon Him do we rely, to Him we do turn, and to Him is our journeying."

As we said, the entire address from beginning to end is addressed to the 'ulamā. There is no indication that the person intended by the expression "those knowledgeable about God" are the Imāms ('a). They are the scholars of Islam, the rabbāniyyūn. The designation rabbāni refers to one who believes in God, fulfills God's ordinances, and is knowledgeable concerning those ordinances, as a trustee of God's decrees concerning what is permitted and what is forbidden.

When the Imām ('a) said that the conduct of affairs belongs to the 'ulamā, he did not mean to restrict this function to a period of ten or twenty years, or simply to the city and people of Medina. It is apparent from the whole speech that his meaning was more universal, that he had in mind a vast community that would undertake the establishment of justice.

If the 'ulamā who are the trustees of God's decrees concerning what is permitted and what is forbidden, and who possess the two characteristics of knowledge and justice as set forth above—if they were to implement God's ordinances, to execute the penal provisions of the law, and generally to conduct and administer the affairs of the

Muslims, the people would no longer be hungry and wretched and the laws of Islam would no longer be in abeyance.

The tradition containing this noble speech, then, is part of the evidence supporting our thesis, the governance of the *faqīh*. Were its chain of transmission not weak, we could cite it as a direct proof. Even as it stands, we might say that the content of the tradition, being veracious, bears witness that it was uttered by one of the *ma'sūmīn*.[313]

We have now completed our discussion of the governance of the *faqīh*; we have nothing further to say on the subject. There is no need to go into details such as the manner in which *zakāt* is to be collected or spent, or how the penal provisions of the law are to be implemented. We have set forth the main principles of the subject and shown that the same governance that was exercised by the Most Noble Messenger (s), and by the Imāms ('a), is also the prerogative of the fuqahā. There can be no doubt about this. If there is any evidence, however, that in certain specific cases the *faqīh* does not possess the same right of governance, we naturally exclude such cases from the operation of the general rule.

As I stated previously, the subject of the governance of *faqīh* is not something new that I have invented; since the very beginning, it has been mentioned continually.

The ruling given by the late Mīrzā Hasan Shirāzi[314] prohibiting the use of tobacco was in effect a governmental ruling; hence all other *fuqahā* were obliged to follow it, and indeed the great *'ulamā* of Iran did follow it, with only a few exceptions. It was not a judicial ruling on a matter being disputed by a few individuals, based purely on his own determination. It was instead a governmental ruling based on the interests of Islam and the Muslims and his determination of a secondary consideration (*'unvān-i-sanavi*).[315] As long as this secondary consideration obtained, the ruling retained its validity, and when the consideration no longer applied, the decree also ceased to apply.

Again, when Mīrzā Muhammad Taqi Shirāzi[316] gave orders for *jihād*—or "defense," they called it—all the *'ulamā* obeyed, because his order was a governmental ruling.

It is related that the late Kāshif al-Ghitā[317] also used to expound much of what I have said. Among other modern scholars, the late Narāqi also was of the opinion that the *fuqahā* are entitled to exercise all the worldly functions of the Most Noble Messenger

---

[313] *Ma'sūmīn*: those possessing the quality of *'ismat* (see n. 67 above); i.e., the Prophet, Fātimah, and the Twelve Imāms. See *A Brief History of the Fourteen Infallibles* (Tehran: WOFIS); Sayyid Murtadā al-'Askari, *The Twelve Successors of the Holy Prophet (s)* [Pub.]

[314] Mīrzā Hasan Shirāzi: a *mujtahid*, d. 1312/1894. After the production and marketing of tobacco in Iran had been made the monopoly of a British company, he declared in December 1891 that "the use of tobacco is tantamount to war against the Imām of the Age." In obedience to his declaration, all of Iran boycotted tobacco, forcing the cancellation of the concession in early 1892. See Algar, *Religion and State*, pp. 205-215.

[315] "Secondary consideration": *'unvān-i sanavi*, a contingent circumstance of legal significance. Tobacco as a substance was religiously unobjectionable; it was the circumstance of the British monopoly that furnished the legal grounds for its prohibition.

[316] Mīrzā Muhammad Taqi Shirāzi: a pupil of Mīrzā Hasan and an important Shī'ah scholar, d. 1338/1921. He was a leading force in the resistance by the Shī'ah *'ulamā* opposed to the imposition of British rule on Iraq at the end of World War I. See Muhammad Hirz ad-Dīn, *Ma'ārif ar-Rijāl* (Najaf, 1384/1964), II, 215-218.

[317] Kāshif al-Ghitā: more fully, Muhammad Husayn Kāshif al-Ghitā, a leading Shī'ah scholar of Iraq, 1295/1876-1373-1954. He was active politically as well as academically throughout his life. See the biographical introduction to his *Asl ash-Shī'ah wa Usūluhā*, 7th ed. (Beirut, 1377/1957), pp. 7-21. The book is translated into English as *The Origin of Shī'ite Islam and Its Principles* (Qum: Ansariyan Publications). [Pub.]

(s). The late Nā'ini also believed that the doctrine of the governance of the *faqīh* may be deduced from the *maqbūla* of 'Umar ibn Hanzalah.[318]

In any case, this subject is by no means new. I have simply examined it at greater length with reference to the different branches of government, to give the subject greater clarity for my listeners. In accordance with the commands of God Almighty, as expressed in His Book and by the tongue of His Most Noble Messenger (s), I have also set forth certain matters of importance to the present age.

We have stressed the main principles of the subject. Now it is up to the present and future generation to discuss it further and reflect upon it, and to find a way to translate it into reality, eschewing all forms of apathy, weakness and despair. God Almighty willing, by means of mutual consultation and the exchange of views, they will develop a method for establishing an Islamic government with all its various branches and departments. They will entrust the affairs of government to persons who are honest, intelligent, believing, and competent and remove traitors from the control of the government, the homeland, and the treasury of the Muslims. Let them be assured that God Almighty is with them.

---

[318] See p. 79.

PROGRAM FOR THE ESTABLISHMENT
OF AN ISLAMIC GOVERNMENT

IT IS OUR DUTY TO WORK toward the establishment of an Islamic government. The first activity we must undertake in this respect is the propagation of our case; that is how we must begin.

It has always been that way, all over the world: a group of people came together, deliberated, made decisions, and then began to propagate their aims. Gradually, the number of like-minded people would increase, until finally they became powerful enough to influence a great state or even to confront and overthrow it, as was the case with the downfall of Muhammad 'Alī Mīrzā and the supplanting of his absolute monarchy with constitutional government.[319] Such movements began with no troops or armed power at their disposal; they always had to resort to propagating the aims of their movement first. The thievery and tyranny practiced by the regime would be condemned and the people awakened and made to understand that the thievery inflicted on them was wrong. Gradually, the scope of this activity would be expanded until it came to embrace all groups of society, and the people, awakened and active, would attain their goal.

You have neither a country nor an army now, but propagating activity is possible for you, because the enemy has been unable to deprive you of all the required means.

You teach the people matters relating to worship, of course, but more important are the political, economic, and legal aspects of Islam. These are, or should be, the focus of our concern. It is our duty to begin exerting ourselves now in order to establish a truly Islamic government. We must propagate our cause to the people, instruct them in it, and convince them of its validity. We must generate a wave of intellectual awakening, to emerge as a current throughout society, and gradually, to take shape as organized Islamic movement made up of the awakened, committed, and religious masses who will rise up and establish an Islamic government.

Propagation and instruction, then, are our two fundamental and most important activities. It is the duty of the *fuqahā* to promulgate religion and instruct the people in the creed, ordinances, and institutions of Islam, in order to pave the way in society for the implementation of Islamic law and the establishment of Islamic institutions. In one of the traditions we have cited, you will have noticed that the successors of the Most Noble Messenger (s) are described as "teaching the people"—that is, instructing them in religion.

This duty is particularly important under the present circumstances, for the imperialists, the oppressive and treacherous rulers, the Jews, Christians, and materialists are all attempting to distort the truths of Islam and lead the Muslims astray. Our responsibilities of propagation and instruction are greater than ever before. We see today that the Jews (may God curse them) have meddled with the text of the Qur'an and have made certain changes in the Qur'ans they have printed in the

---

[319] On June 23, 1908, Muhammad 'Alī Shāh carried out with Russian aid a military coup against the first Iranian Majlis. He was overthrown and constitutional rule restored on July 16, 1909, as a result of popular resistance, largely directed by the most important religious scholars of the day in Najaf. See Browne, *The Persian Revolution of 1905-1909*, chs. 7-10.

occupied territories.[320] It is our duty to prevent this treacherous interference with the text of Qur'an. We must protest and make the people aware that the Jews and their foreign backers are opposed to the very foundations of Islam and wish to establish Jewish domination throughout the world. Since they are a cunning and resourceful group of people, I fear that —God forbid— they may one day achieve their goal, and that the apathy shown by some of us may allow a Jew to rule over us one day. May God never let us see such a day!

At the same time, a number of orientalists serving as propaganda agents for the imperialist institution are also active in endeavors to distort and misrepresent the truths of Islam. The agents of imperialism are busy in every corner of the Islamic world drawing our youth from us with their evil propaganda. They are not converting them into Jews and Christians; they are corrupting them, making them irreligious and indifferent, which is sufficient for their purposes. In our own city of Tehran now there are centers of evil propaganda run by the churches, the Zionists, and the Bahā'is in order to lead our people astray and make them abandon the ordinances and teachings of Islam. Do we not have a duty to destroy these centers that are damaging Islam? Is it enough for us simply to possess Najaf? (Actually, we do not even have Najaf!)[321] Should we be content to sit lamenting in Qum, or should we come to life and be active?

You, the younger generation in the religious institution, must come fully to life and keep the command of God alive. Develop and refine your thinking, and lay aside your concern with the minutiae and subtleties of the religious sciences, because that kind of concentration on petty detail has kept many of us from performing our more important duties. Come to the aid of Islam; save Islam! They are destroying Islam! Invoking the laws of Islam and the name of the Most Noble Messenger (s), they are destroying Islam! Agents—both foreigners sent by the imperialists and natives employed by them—have spread out into every village and region of Iran and are leading our children and young people astray, who might otherwise be of service to Islam one day. Help save our young people from this danger!

It is your duty to disseminate among the people the religious knowledge you have acquired and to acquaint them with the subjects you have learned. The scholar or the *faqīh* is accorded praise and glorified in the traditions because he is the one who makes the ordinances, doctrines, and institutions of Islam known to the people and instructs them in the Sunnah of the Most Noble Messenger (s). You must now devote your energies to the tasks of propagation and instruction in order to present Islam more fully to the people.

It is our duty to dispel the doubts about Islam that have been created; until we have erased these doubts from people's minds, we will not be able to accomplish anything. We must impress upon ourselves and upon the generation—and even the generation after that—the necessity for dispelling these doubts about Islam that have arisen in the

---

[320] Soon after the Six-Day War, it was reported that copies of the Qur'an were circulating in the territories seized by the Zionists, as well as in African countries, from which all verses critical of the Jews had been excised.

[321] Najaf is the main center of learning in the Shī'i world. The lament here that "we do not even have Najaf" refers to the restrictions and pressure placed on the Shī'ah scholars of Najaf by the Ba'athist regime of Baghdad. The Ba'athist persecution of Najaf reached a highpoint in May 1969—ten months before these lectures were given—when a number of 'ulamā were arrested and tortured and religious endowments were confiscated. See anon., *Hayāt-e-Kareem*, in Eng. (Karachi, 1973), pp. 73-84. After the victory of the Islamic Revolution in Iran, the crime of the regime in Baghdad was epitomized by torturing and cold-bloodedly murdering Āyatullāh al-'Uzma Sayyid Muhammad al-Bāqir as-Sadr and his sister Bint al-Hudā in April 1980. [Pub.]

minds of many people, even the educated among us, as the result of centuries of false propaganda. You must acquaint the people with the worldview, social institution, and form of government proposed by Islam, so that they may come to know what Islam is and what its laws are.

It is the duty of the teaching institution today in Qum, Mashhad, and elsewhere to propagate Islam, to expound this faith and school of thought. In addition to Islam, you must make yourselves known to the people of the world and also authentic models of Islamic leadership and government. You must address yourselves to the university people in particular, the educated class. The students have had their eyes opened. I assure you that if you present Islam and Islamic government to the universities accurately, the students will welcome it and accept it. The students are opposed to tyranny; they are opposed to the puppet regimes imperialism imposes; they are opposed to thievery and the plundering of public wealth; they are opposed to this consumption of what is forbidden and this deceitful propaganda. But no student could be opposed to Islam, whose form of government and teachings are beneficial to society. The students are looking to Najaf, appealing for help. Should we sit idle, waiting for them to enjoin the good upon us and call us to our duties?[322] Our young people studying in Europe are enjoining the good upon us; say to us: "We have organized Islamic associations; now help us!"[323]

It is our duty to bring all these matters to the attention of the people. We must explain what the form of government is in Islam and how rule was conducted in the earliest days of Islamic history. We must tell them how the center of command and the seat of the judiciary under it were both located in part of the mosque, at a time when the Islamic state embraced the farthest reaches of Iran, Egypt, the Hijaz, and the Yemen. Unfortunately, when government passed into the hands of the next generations, it was converted into a monarchy, or even worse than a monarchy.

The people must be instructed in these matters and helped to mature, intellectually and politically. We must tell them what kind of government we want, what kinds of people would assume responsibility for affairs in the government we propose, and what policies and programs they would follow. The ruler in Islamic society is a person who treats his brother 'Aqil[324] in such a way that he would never request extra support from the public treasury (lest there be economic discrimination among the Muslims), and who requires to account for the guaranteed loan she has obtained from the public treasury, telling her, "If you do not pay back this loan, you will be the be the first woman of the Bani Hāshim[325] to have her hand cut off." That is the kind of ruler and leader we want, a leader who will put the law into practice instead of his personal desires and inclinations; who will treat all members of the community as equals before the law; who will refuse to countenance privilege or discrimination in any form; who will place his own family on an equal footing with the rest of the people;

---

[322] Insofar as the "enjoining of the good" is the particular duty of the religious scholars, it would be shaming for them to need a reminder from students.

[323] Throughout his exile in Najaf, Imām Khomeini gave special attention to the Islamic associations of Iranian students in Europe and the United States, sending them guidance and encouragement. For an example of his messages to the Iranian Muslim students in North America, see *Islam and Revolution*, pp. 209-211.

[324] 'Āqil ibn Abi Tālib: brother of Imām 'Ali. After Imām 'Ali assumed the caliphate, 'Aqil is related to have asked him to withdraw 40,000 dirhams from the public treasury to enable him to settle a debt. When his request was denied, 'Aqil abandoned his brother and joined the camp of Mu'āwiyah in Damascus.

[325] Bani Hāshim: the Meccan clan to which the Prophet and his descendants belonged. See Subhāni, chap. 4, "Ancestors of the Prophet," [Pub.]

who will cut off the hand of his own son if he commits a theft; who will execute his own brother and sister if they sell heroin (not execute people for possession of ten grams of heroin when his own relative operate gangs that bring into the country heroin by the hundred-weight).[326]

Many of the ordinances of Islam that refer to worship also pertain to social and political functions. The forms of worship practiced in Islam are usually linked to politics and the gestation of society. For example, congregational prayer, the gathering on the occasion of *hajj*, and Friday prayer, for all their spirituality, exert a political as well as moral and doctrinal influence. Islam has provided for such gatherings so that religious use might be made of them; so that feelings of brotherhood and cooperation may be strengthened, intellectual maturity fostered, solutions found for political and social problems, with *jihad* and collective effort as the natural outcome.

In non-Islamic countries, or Islamic countries ruled by non-Islamic governments, whenever they want the people to assemble like this, millions must be spent out of the national treasury or budget, and even then the result is unsatisfactory; such meetings lack spontaneity and spirit and are of no real consequence. In Islam, however, anyone who wishes to perform the *hajj* departs of his own will and goes on the *hajj*. Also people go eagerly to take part in congregational prayer. We must take advantage of these assemblies to propagate and teach religion and to develop the ideological and political movement of Islam.

Some people are completely unaware of this; they are only concerned about the correct pronunciation of *"wa lā 'dh-dhāllīn."*[327] When they go on the *hajj*, instead of exchanging ideas with their Muslim brothers, propagating the beliefs and ordinances of Islam, and seeking solutions to the universal problems and afflictions of the Muslims (for example, rallying to liberate Palestine, which is part of the Islamic homeland)—instead of doing all this, they exacerbate the differences that exist among Muslims. The first Muslims, on the other hand, used to accomplish important business on the occasion of *hajj* or at their Friday gatherings. The Friday sermon was more than a *sūrah* from the Qur'an and a prayer followed by a few brief words. Entire armies used to be mobilized by Friday sermon and proceed directly from the mosque to the battlefield—and a man who sets out from the mosque to go into battle will fear only God, not poverty, hardship, or his army will be victorious and triumphant. When you look at the Friday sermons given in that age and the sermons of the Commander of the Faithful ('a), you see that their purpose was to set people in motion, to arouse them to fight and sacrifice themselves for Islam, to resolve the sufferings of the people of this world.

If the Muslims before us had gathered every Friday and reminded themselves of their common problems, and solved them or resolved to solve them, we would not be in the position we find ourselves in today. Today we must start organizing these assemblies in earnest and make use of them for the sake of propagation and instruction. The

---

[326] An allusion to the activities of Ashraf, the Shāh's twin sister, who was reported in 1960 to have been detained by the Swiss police after large quantities of heroin were found in her possession. See Bahman Nīrūmand, *Persien, Modell eines Entwicklungslandes* (Hamburg, 1967), pp. 133-134.

[327] *Wa lā 'adh-Dhāllīn*: "not those who go astray," a phrase occurring in the seventh verse of the opening chapter of the Qur'an that is recited in every prayer. The letter *dh* (ض) in *'dh-dhāllīn* represents an Arabic sound that does not exist in Persian and it is generally pronounced by Persian speakers as a *z*. Nonetheless, there are those—in Iran and elsewhere—who devote excessive energy to the task of giving the letter its Arabic value when reciting the verse in prayer.

ideological and political movement of Islam will thus develop and advance toward its climax.

Make Islam known to the people, then, and in so doing, create something akin to 'Āshūrā.[328] Just as we have steadfastly preserved the awareness of 'Āshūrā (peace be upon its founder) and not let it be lost, so that people still gather during Muharram and beat their breasts, we should now take measures to create a wave of protest against the state of the government; let the people gather, and the preachers and *rawzakhwāns*[329] firmly fix the issue of government in their minds.

If you present Islam accurately and acquaint people with its worldview, doctrines, principles, ordinances, and social system, they will welcome it ardently (God knows, many people want it). I have witnessed that myself. A single word was enough once to cause a wave of enthusiasm among the people, because then, like now, they were all dissatisfied and unhappy with the state of affairs. They are living now in the shadow of the bayonet, and repression will let them say nothing. They want someone to stand up fearlessly and speak out. So, courageous sons of Islam, stand up! Address the people bravely; tell the truth about our situation to the masses in simple language; arouse them to enthusiastic activity, and turn the people in the street and the bazaar, our simple-hearted workers and peasants, and our alert students into dedicated *mujāhids*.[330] The entire population will become *mujāhids*. All segments of society are ready to struggle for the sake of freedom, independence, and the happiness of the nation, and their struggle needs religion. Give the people Islam, then, for Islam is the school of *jihād*, the religion of struggle; let them amend their characters and beliefs in accordance with Islam and transform themselves into a powerful force, so that they may overthrow the tyrannical regime imperialism has imposed on us and set up an Islamic government.

Only those *fuqahā* who make people acquainted with the beliefs and institutions of Islam, and who defend and protect them, are truly "citadels of Islam."[331] They must deliver rousing, impassioned speeches and lead the people in order to fulfill this function. Only then, if they live to be, say, 120, will the people feel that Islam has suffered a misfortune with their passing away and that a gap has appeared in the Muslim community, or as the tradition puts it, "A crack will appear in the fortress of Islam." Will some irremediable deficiency occur in Islamic society now if one of us dies after spending his life at home reading books? What loss could our death mean? But when Islam lost Imām Husayn ('a), then indeed the loss was irreparable. A loss occurs with the death of people who have preserved the doctrines, laws, and social institutions of Islam, like Khwājah Nāsir ad-Dīn Tūsi[332] or 'Allāmah Hilli.[333] But

---

[328] 'Āshūrā: the tenth day of Muharram; the day on which Imām Husayn was martyred in Karbala. See n. 11 above.

[329] *Rauzakwāns*: those who specialize in reciting narrations, often versified, of the martyrdom of the Imāms. The first part of the designation, *rauza*, is taken from the title of one such narrative, *Rauzat ash-Shuhadā*, by Husayn Vā'iz Khāshifi (d. 910/1504).

[330] *Mujāhid*: those who engage in *jihād*, who struggle for the attainment of God's purposes on earth.

[331] "Citadels of Islam": see the tradition cited on p. 58.

[332] Khwāja Nāsir ad-Dīn Tūsi: one of the most outstanding of all Shī'ah scholars, 597/1201-672/1274. He wrote voluminously not only on the religious sciences, but also on philosophy, mathematics, and astronomy. He joined the entourage of the Mongol conqueror Hulagu when he was passing through Iran on his way to Baghdad, a circumstance that has led many to accuse him of complicity in the conquest. Concerning his associations with the Mongols, see A.H. Hā'iri, "Nāsir ad-Dīn Tūsi: His Alleged Role in the Fall of Baghdad," *Actes du Ve Congress international d'Arabisants et d'Islamisants* (Brussels, 1971), pp. 255-266.

what have you or I done for Islam that our passing should remind men of that tradition? If a thousand of us were to die, nothing would happen. The only explanation for this is that either we are not true *fuqahā* or we are not true believers.

No reasonable person expects our activities of propagation and instruction to lead quickly to the formation of an Islamic government. In order to succeed in establishing an Islamic government, we must have several kinds of continuous activities. Ours is a goal that will take time to achieve. Sensible people in this world lay one stone in position on the ground in the hope that someone two hundred years later will come to finish a building mounted upon it so that the goal will finally be reached. Once the caliph said to an old man who was planting a walnut tree: "Old man! Why plant this walnut tree, which will not bear fruit until fifty years from now, by which time you will be dead?" The man replied: "Others planted so that we might eat. We are planting so that others may eat."

We must preserve in our efforts even though they may not yield their result until the next generation, for our service is devoted to Islam and the cause of human happiness. If it were for a personal cause, we might say: "Why trouble ourselves! Our efforts cannot benefit us, but only those who come later." If the Doyen of the Martyrs ('a), who risked and indeed sacrificed all his material interests, had thought that way, acting only for himself and his personal benefits, he would have compromised with Yazīd[334] at the very beginning and settled the whole affair—the Umayyad rulers were only too anxious for him to swear allegiance to them and accept them as rulers. What could have been better for them than to have the grandson of the Prophet (s), the Imām of the Age, call them "Commander of the Faithful" and recognize their rule? But his concern was the future of Islam and the Muslims. So that Islam might be propagated among men in the future, and its political and social order established in society, he opposed the Umayyads, fought against them, and ultimately sacrificed himself.

Examine carefully one of the traditions I have cited above. You will see that Imām as-Sādiq ('a) was subjected to pressure by oppressive rulers and therefore chose *taqiyyah*. He had no executive power, and most of the time he was confined under surveillance. Nevertheless, he kept informing the Muslims of their duties and appointing judges for them. What was the reason for this, and what benefit was there in appointing and dismissing judges?

Great men, with broad horizons of thought, never despair or pay attention to the circumstances in which they find themselves—imprisonment or captivity, for example, which may continue indefinitely; instead, they continue making plans for the advancement of their cause. Either they will carry out their plans themselves, or if they are not granted the opportunity, others will follow their plans, even if it is two or three hundred years later. The foundations of many great movements in history were laid in this way. Sukarno, the former president of Indonesia, conceived and drew up his plans in prison and later put them into practice.

Imām as-Sādiq ('a) not only laid down plans; he also made appointments to certain posts. If his appointments had been intended for that time, naturally they would have been pointless, but in reality, he was thinking of the future. He was not like us, thinking only of ourselves and concerned with our personal predicaments; he was concerned with the *ummah*, with humanity as a whole, and he wished to reform

---

[333] 'Allāmah Hilli: more fully, 'Allāmah ibn al-Mutahhar al-Hilli, another important Shī'ah scholar who lived in the period of Mongol domination of Iran, 648/1250-716/1325. Concerning his scholarly and political activities, see Michel Mazzaoui, *The Rise of the Safawids* (Wiesbaden, 1972), pp. 27-34.
[334] Yazid: second Umayyad caliph and adversary of Imām Husayn. He ruled from 60/680-64/683.

mankind by implementing the laws of justice. Thus, more than a thousand years ago, he had to lay down a pattern of government and make his appointments, so that on the day when the nations awoke and the Muslims came to their senses, there would be no confusion and the form of Islamic government and its leadership would be known.

Generally speaking, Islam, and the Shī'i school of thought, and indeed, all religions and schools of thought have advanced and progressed in this fashion. They all started with nothing but a plan, which came to fruition later because of the fortitude and dedication of the respective leaders and prophets.

Moses was a mere shepherd, and for years he followed that calling. When he was summoned to do battle with the pharaoh, he had no supporter or helper. But as a result of his innate ability and his steadfastness, he overthrew the rule of the pharaoh with a staff. Now imagine that staff in the hands of you or me would we have been able to achieve the same result? It takes the determination, seriousness, and resourcefulness of a Moses to make that staff capable of overthrowing a pharaoh; not everyone can perform such a feat.

When the Most Noble Messenger (s) was given his prophetic mission and began to propagate his massage, an eight-year old child (the Commander of the Faithful, upon whom be peace) and a forty-year old woman (his wife Khadījah) were the only people who believed in him; he had no one else. Everyone knows of the vexations that plagued the Prophet, the obstacles that were placed in his way, the oppositions that he faced. Yet he never despaired or said, "I am all alone." He persisted and, with his spiritual power and firm resolve, was able to advance his cause from nothing to the point it has reached today, where seven hundred million people are gathered under his banner.

The Shī'i school of thought also began from zero. On the day that the Most Noble Messenger (s) laid its foundations, he was greeted with mockery. He invited people to his house and told them, "The man who possesses such-and-such qualities is to be my minister," meaning the Commander of the Faithful ('a). At the time, the Commander of the Faithful had not yet reached adulthood, although he always possessed a great spirit, the greatest in the world. But no one rose to pay him respect, and some one even turned to Abū Tālib[335] and said to him in jest, "You are to march under the banner of your son now!"

Also on the day of the Prophet's announcement to the people that the Commander of the Faithful ('a) was to succeed him and govern, some expressed apparent admiration and satisfaction, but the opposition to him began on that very day and continued down to the end. If the Most Noble Messenger (s), had appointed him only as an authority to be consulted on legal problems, there would have been no opposition to him. Since he assigned him the rank of successor, however, and said that he was to rule over Muslims and be entrusted with the destiny of the Islamic nation, various sorts of discontent and opposition arose. If you, too, were to sit at home today, and not intervene in the affairs of the country, no one would disturb you. They trouble you only when you try to intervene in the destiny of the nation. It was because they intervened in the affairs of government and the country that the Commander of the Faithful and his followers were harassed and persecuted. But they did not abandon their activity and their struggle, with the result that today, thanks to their labors, there are about two hundred million Shī'ah in the world.

---

[335] Abū Tālib: father of Imām 'Ali. According to Shī'i belief, he embraced Islam; but according to Sunni belief, he did not. For a discussion of his faith in Islam, see Subhāni, *op. cit.*, chap. 21, "Death of Abū Tālib," *Islam of Abū Tālib (Part I-IV)* [Pub.]

To present Islam properly to the people, the religious teaching institutions must be reformed. The syllabi and methods of propagation and instruction must be improved; apathy, laziness, despair, and lack of self-confidence must be replaced by diligence, endeavor, hope and self-confidence; the effects left on the minds of some people by foreigners' insinuating propaganda must be erased; the attitudes of the pseudo-saintly persons, who, despite their position within the teaching institution, make it difficult for people to gain a true appreciation of Islam and the necessity for social reforms, must be changed; and the court-affiliated ākhūnds,[336] who have sold their religion for worldly gain, must be divested of their garb and expelled from the religious institution.

The agents of imperialism, together with the educational and political apparatuses of the anti-national puppet governments they have installed, have been spreading poison for centuries and corrupting the minds and morals of the people. Those who have entered the religious institutions have naturally brought with them traces of this corruption, for the religious institution make up part of society and the people. We must therefore strive to reform, intellectually and morally, the members of the religious institution and to remove the traces left on their minds and spirits by the insinuating propaganda of the foreigners and the policies of corrupt and treacherous governments.

One can easily observe the effects of which I speak. For example, sometimes I see people who sit in the centers of religious institution saying to each other, "These matters are beyond us; what business are they of ours? All we are supposed to do is to offer our prayers and to give our opinions on questions of religious law." Ideas like these are the result of several centuries of malicious propaganda on the part of the imperialists penetrating deeply into the very heart of Najaf, Qum, Mashhad, and other religious centers, causing apathy, depression, and laziness to appear; and preventing people from maturing, so that they constantly make excuses for themselves and say, "These matters are beyond us!"

These ideas are wrong. What are the qualifications of those who now rule the Muslims countries? What gives them the ability to rule that we allegedly lack? Who among them has any more ability than the average person? Many of them have never studies anything! Where did the ruler of the Hijāz ever go to study? As for Rizā Khān, he was totally illiterate, an illiterate soldier, no more! It has been the same throughout history: many arbitrary and tyrannical rulers have been totally lacking in any capacity to govern the society or administer the nation and devoid of learning and accomplishment. What did Hārūn ar-Rashīd[337] ever study, or any other man who ruled over realms as vast as his? Study—the acquisition of knowledge and expertise in various science—is necessary for making plans for a country and for exercising executive and administrative functions; we too will make use of people with those qualifications. But as for the supervision and supreme administration of the country, the dispensing of justice, and the establishment of equitable relations among the people—these are precisely the subjects that the *faqīh* has studied. Whatever is needed to preserve national independence and liberty is, again, precisely what the *faqīh* has to offer. For it is the *faqīh*, who refuses to submit to others or fall under the influence of foreigners, and who defends the rights of the nation and the freedom, independence, and territorial integrity of the Islamic homeland, even at the cost of his life. It is the *faqīh*, who does not deviate either to the left or to the right.

---

[336] *Ākhūnd*: see n. 5 above.
[337] Hārūn ar-Rashīd: Abbasid caliph who reigned from 180/186-193/809 and was the contemporary of the seventh and eighth Imāms, Mūsā al-Kāzim and Ridā.

Rid yourselves of your depression and apathy. Improve your methods and program of propagation, try diligently to present Islam accurately, and resolve to establish an Islamic government. Assume the lead and join hands with the militant and freedom-loving people. An Islamic government will definitely be established; have confidence in yourselves. You have the power, courage, and sense of strategy it takes to struggle for national liberty and independence, you have succeeded in waking the people and inspiring them to struggle, casing imperialism and tyranny to tremble. Day by day, you are accumulating more experience and your ability to deal with the affairs of society is increasing. Once you have succeeded in overthrowing the tyrannical regimes, you will certainly be capable of administering the state and guiding the masses.

The entire system of government and administration, together with the necessary laws, lies ready for you. If the administration of the country calls for taxes, Islam has made the necessary provision; and if laws are needed, Islam has established them all. There is no need for you, after establishing a government, to sit down and draw up laws, or, like rulers who worship foreigners and are infatuated with the West, run after others to borrow their laws. Everything is ready and waiting. All that remains is to draw up ministerial programs, and that can be accomplished with the help and cooperation of consultants and advisers who are experts in different fields, gathered together in a consultative assembly.

Fortunately, the Muslim peoples are ready to follow you and your allies. What we are lacking are the necessary resolve and armed power, and these, too, we shall acquire, God willing. We need the staff of Moses and the resolve of Moses; we need people who are able to wield the staff of Moses and the sword of the Commander of the Faithful ('a).

But the gutless people who now sit in the religious centers are certainly not capable of establishing and maintaining a government; for they are so gutless that they cannot wield even a pen or undertake any activity at all. The foreigners and their agents have filled our ears with their propaganda so often that we have begun to believe we are incapable of anything: "Go mind your own business! Attend to your schools, your classes, your studies. What business of yours are these matters? They are beyond your capacity!" I cannot disabuse some people of these notions and make them understand that they must become leaders of humanity; that they are at least the equals of others and are capable of administrating the country. What qualifications do others have that they lack? All one can say is that some of the others went abroad to enjoy themselves, and maybe studied a little while they were there. (We do not say they should not study. We are not opposed to study or learning. Let them go to the moon, found an atomic industry; we will not stand in their way. However, we have duties as well.)

Give them Islam; proclaim to the world the program of Islamic government; maybe the kings and presidents of the Muslim countries will understand the truth of what we say and accept it. We would not want to take any thing away from them; we will leave anyone in his place who faithfully follows Islam.

Today, we have 700 million Muslims in the world, 170 million or more of whom are Shī'ah. They are all ready to follow us, but we are so lacking in resolve that we are unable to lead them. We must establish a government that will enjoy the trust of the people, one in which the people have confidence and to which they will be able to entrust their destiny. We need trustworthy rulers who will guard the trust the people have placed with them, so that protected by them and the law, the peoples will be able to live their lives and go about their tasks in tranquility. These are the things to which you should be devoting your thought. Do not despair; do not imagine that this task is impossible. God knows that your capacity and courage are not less than those of others—unless, of course, the meaning of courage is oppressing and slaughtering the people; that kind of courage we certainly do not have.

Once that man came to see me while I was in prison[338] along with Āqā-yi Qummi[339] (may God preserve him), who is under arrest again now. He said: "Politics is all dirt, lying, and viciousness; why don't you leave it to us?"

What he said was true in a sense; if that is what politics really consists of, it belongs exclusively to them. But the politics of Islam, of the Muslims, of the guiding Imāms who lead God's servants by means of politics, is quite different from the politics he was speaking of.

Afterwards, he told the newspapers: "An agreement has been reached to the effect that the religious leaders will not interfere in politics." As soon as I was released, I denied his statement from the *minbar*. I said: "He is lying; if Khomeini or anyone else gives such a pledge, he will be expelled from the religious institution!"[340]

At the outset, they plant in your minds the suggestion that politics means lying and the like so that you lose all interest in national affairs and they can proceed with their business undisturbed, doing whatever they like and indulging all their vices. Meanwhile, you are to sit here offering prayers for their welfare: "May God perpetuate their rule!" They, of course, do not have the intelligence to elaborate such a plan themselves (thank God!); it is their masters and the experts who advise them that devised this plan. The British imperialists penetrated the countries of the East more than three hundred years ago. Being knowledgeable about all aspects of these countries, they drew up elaborate plans for assuming control of them. Then came the new imperialists, the Americans and others. They allied themselves with the British and took part in the execution of their plans.

Once when I was in Hamadān, a former student of the religious sciences, who had forsaken the religious garb but preserved his Islamic ethics, came to see me and he showed me a map on which certain places had been marked in red. He told me that those red symbols indicated all the mineral resources existing in Iran that had been located by foreign experts.

Foreign experts have studied our country, and have discovered all our mineral reserves—gold, copper, petroleum, and so on. They have also made an assessment of our people's intelligence and came to the conclusion that the only barriers blocking their way are Islam and the religious leadership.

They have known the power of Islam themselves for it once ruled part of Europe, and they know that true Islam is opposed to their activities. They have also realized they cannot make the true religious scholars submit to their influence, nor can they affect their thinking. From the very outset, therefore, they have sought to remove this obstacle from their path by disparaging Islam and besmirching the religious leaders. They have resorted to malicious propaganda so that today, we imagine that Islam simply consists of a handful of legal topics. They have also tried to destroy the reputation of *fuqahā* and the *'ulamā*, who stand at the head of Islam society, by

---

[338] "That man" was Hasan Pakravan, head of SAVAK between 1961 and 1965, executed after the triumph of the Islamic Revolution. This visit occurred on July 2, 1963 when Imām Khomeini was being detained at the 'Ashratābād garrison in Tehran. See S.H.R., *Barrasī va Tahlīlī*, p. 575.

[339] Āqā-yi Qummi: that is, Āyatullāh Hasan Tabātabā'i Qummi, religious leader of Mashhad who actively cooperated with Imām Khomeini in the movement of Khurdād 15.

[340] For the text of this speech, given at the Masjid-i A'zam in Qum on March 6, 1964, see anon., *Biyūgrāfi-yi Pīshvā*, n.p., n.d., II, 109-138; *Sahīfeh-ye Imām* (Tehran: The Institute for Compilation and Publication of Imam Khomeini's Works, 1379 Sh.), vol. 1, p. 269. [Pub.]

slanderous accusations and other means. For example, that shameless agent of imperialism wrote in his book[341]: "Six hundred of the *'ulamā* of Najaf and Iran were on the payroll of the British. Shaykh Murtadā[342] took the money for only two years before he realized where it was coming from. The proof may be found in documents preserved in the India Office archives." Imperialism tells him to insult the *'ulamā* so that it may reap the benefits. Imperialism dearly wants to present all the *'ulamā* as being on its payroll so that they will lose the respect of the people and the people will turn away from them. At the same time, they have tried with their propaganda and insinuations to present Islam as a petty, limited affair, and to restrict the functions of the *fuqahā* and *'ulamā* to insignificant matters. They have constantly tried to persuade us that the only duty of the *fuqahā* is to give their opinion on legal problems.

Some people, lacking in correct understanding, have believed them and gone astray. They have failed to realize that all this is part of a plan designed to destroy our independence and establish control over all aspects of life in the Islamic countries. Unwittingly, they have assisted the propaganda organs of imperialism in carrying out its politics and reaching its goals. The propaganda institutions of imperialism have sought to persuade us that religion must be separate from politics, that the religious leaders must not interfere in social matters, and that the *fuqahā* do not have the duty of overseeing the destiny of the Islamic nation. Unfortunately, some people have believed them and fallen under their influence, with the result that we see. This result is what the imperialists have always desired, desire now, and will desire in the future.

Look at the religious teaching centers and you will see the effects of this imperialist propaganda. You will see negligent, lazy, idle, and apathetic people who do nothing but discuss points of law and offer their prayers, and are incapable of anything else. You will also encounter ideas and habits that are born of the same imperialist propaganda—for example, the idea that to speak is incompatible with the dignity of the *ākhūnd*; the *ākhūnd* and the *mujtahīd* should not be able to speak, or if they are, they should not say anything except, "*Lā ilāha illa 'Llāh*," or may be one word more! But that is wrong, and contrary to the Sunnah of God's Messenger (s). God has praised speech and expression, as well as writing and the use of pen. For example, He says in *Sūrat ar-Rahmān*: "He taught him [man] expression" (55: 4), counting the instruction in speech that He gave man as a great blessing and a source of nobility. Speech and expression are necessary for promulgating the ordinances of God and the teachings and doctrines of Islam; it is by means of them that we can instruct the people in their religion and fulfill the duty indicated in the phrase: "They instruct the people."[343] The Most Noble Messenger and the Commander of Faithful both delivered speeches and sermons; they were men of eloquence.

These foolish ideas that exist in the minds of some people help the imperialists and the oppressive governments in their attempts to keep the Muslim countries in their present state and to block the progress of the Islamic movement. Such ideas are characteristic of those who are known as saintly but in reality are pseudo-saints, not true ones. We must change the way they think and make clear our attitudes toward

---

[341] The reference may be to a passage in Mahmūd Mahmūd, *Tārīkh-i Ravābit-i Siyāsī-yi Īrān va Inglīs* (Tehran, 1332 Sh./1953), VI, 1743. Sultān Ghāzī ad-Dīn Haydar of Oudh established an endowment of a hundred lakhs of rupees for the support of the needy in Najaf and Karbala. After his principality was absorbed into British India, the administration of the endowment passed into British hands. Concerning the Oudh bequest and its recipients, see Algar, *Religion and State*, pp. 237-238.

[342] Shaykh Murtadā: that is, Shaykh Murtadā Ansārī, first *mujtahid* to become the sole source of guidance (*marja'-i taqlīd*) of the Shī'i world, 1216/1801-1281/1865. He was the author of *al-Makāsib*, a major work on Shī'i jurisprudence. See Algar, *Religion and State*, pp. 162-164.

[343] See p.52.

them, for they are blocking our movement and the reforms we want to carry out, and are keeping our hands tied.

The late Burūjirdī,[344] the late Hujjat,[345] the late Sadr,[346] and the late Khwansari[347] (may God be pleased with all of them) had gathered in our house one day to discuss some political matter. I said to them: "Before anything else, you must decide what to do with these pseudo-saints. As long as they are there, our situation is like that of a person who is attacked by an enemy while someone else keeps his hands bound behind him. These persons who are known as saints but are pseudo-saints, not real ones, are totally unaware of the state of society, and if you want to do something—take over the government, assume control of the Majlis, stop the spread of corruption—they will destroy your standing in society. Before everything else, you must decide what to do with them."

The state of Muslim society today is such that these false saints prevent Islam from exerting its proper influence; acting in the name of Islam, they are inflicting damage upon Islam. The roots of this group that exists in our society are to be found in the centers of the religious institution. In the centers at Najaf, Qum, Mashhad, and elsewhere, there are individuals who have this pseudo-saintly mentality, and from their base within the religious institution, they infect the rest of society with their evil ideas and attitudes. They will oppose anyone who tells the people: "Come now, awaken! Let us not live under the banners of others! Let us not be subject to the imposition of Britain and America! Let us not allow Israel to paralyze the Muslims!"

First, we must advise these pseudo-saints and try to awaken them. We must say to them: "Can you not see the danger? Do you not see that the Israelis are attacking, killing, and destroying and the British and Americans are helping them? You sit there watching, but you must wake up; you must try to find a remedy for the ills of the people. Mere discussion is not enough. Simply pronouncing opinions on points of law is of no use by itself. Do not keep silent at a time when Islam is being destroyed, Islam is being wiped out, like Christians who sat discussing the Holy Ghost and the Trinity until they were destroyed.[348] Wake up! Pay some attention to reality and the questions of the day. Do not let yourselves be so negligent. Are you waiting for the angels to come and carry you on their wings? Is it the function of the angles to pamper the idle? The angels spread their wings beneath the feet of the Commander of the Faithful (‘a) because he was of benefit to Islam: he made Islam great, secured the expansion of Islam in the world and promoted its interests. Under his leadership, a free, vital, virtuous society came into being and won fame; everyone had to bow before him its might, even the enemy. But why should anyone bow before you, whose only activity is offering opinions on points of law?

---

[344] Burūjirdi: that is, Āyatullāh Husayn Burūjirdi, concerning whom, see p. xii. See also ‘Abbās al-‘Abīrī, *Āyatullāh Al-Broojerdi*, trans. Muhammad Hasan Najafi (Qum: Ansariyan Publications). [Pub.]

[345] Hujjat: that is, Āyatullāh Muhammad Hujjat, a teacher for many years and an associate of Āyatullāh Hā'iri, 1310/1862-1372/1953. He was responsible for the building of Hujjatiyyah Madrasah. See Muhammad Sharīf Rāzi, *Ganjinā-yi Dānishmandān* (Tehran, 1352 Sh./1973), I, pp. 305-335.

[346] Sadr: that is, Āyatullāh Sadr ad-Dīn, 1299/1882-1373/1953, another of the chief associates of Hā'iri in Qum. See Rāzi, *Ganjinā-yi Dānishmandān*, I, pp. 326-335.

[347] Khwansāri: that is, Āyatullāh Muhammad Taqi Khwansāri, a religious scholar who combined militancy with learning, 1305/1888-1371/1952. He fought against the British occupiers of Iraq under the leadership of Mīrzā Muhammad Taqi Shirāzi (see n. 157) before joining the circle of Hā'iri in Qum. See Rāzi, *Ganjinā-yi Dānishmandān*, I, pp. 322-326; Hasan Iedrem, *Āyatullāh Khonsāri: Through Sources of Witnesses*, trans. ‘Abbās Abū Sa‘eedi (Qum: Ansariyan Publications). [Pub.]

[348] Possibly a reference to the Christological disputes of Byzantium.

If our pseudo-saints do not wake up, and begin to assume their responsibilities after repeated admonition and advice, it will be obvious that the cause of their failure is not ignorance, but something else. Then, of course, we will adopt a different attitude toward them.

The centers of the religious institution are places for teaching, instruction, propagation, and leadership. They belong to the just *fuqahā*, learned scholars, teachers, and students. They belong to those who are the trustees and successors of the prophets. They represent a trust, and it is obvious that a divine trust cannot be placed in the hands of anyone. Whoever wishes to assume such a weighty responsibility, to administer the affairs of the Muslims and to act as the deputy of the Commander of the Faithful ('a), to settle matters concerning the honor, property, and lives of the people, as well as the booty taken in war and the penal provisions of the law—such a person must be totally disinterested in the world and devoid of worldly ambition. Anyone whose efforts are oriented to this world—even in matters that are inherently legitimate—cannot be the trustee of God, and is not worthy of our trust. Any *faqīh* who joins the state apparatus of the oppressors and becomes a hanger-on of the court is not a trustee and cannot exercise God's trust. God knows what misfortunes Islam has suffered—from its inception down to the present at the hands of these evil *'ulamā*! Abū Hurayrah was one of the *fuqahā*, but God knows what judgments he falsified for Mu'āwiyah and others like him, and what damage he inflicted upon Islam. When an ordinary person enters the service of an oppressive government, he is to be accounted a sinner, but no greater harm will come of it. But, when a *faqīh* like Abū Hurayrah[349] or a judge like Shurayh joins such a government, he improves its standing while besmirching the reputation of Islam. When a *faqīh* enters the service of an oppressive government, it is as if the whole *ulamā* entered it along with him; it is no longer a question of a single individual. It is for this reason that the Imāms ('a) strictly forbade their followers to join the government service, and told them that the situation they found themselves in had come about because some of them had done so.

The obligations that are incumbent on the *fuqahā* do not apply to others; on account of their position and function, *fuqahā* must avoid and relinquish even things that are otherwise licit. In cases where others are permitted to resort to *taqiyyah*, *fuqahā* may not. The purpose of *taqiyyah* is the preservation of Islam and the Shī'i school; if people had not resorted to it, our school of thought would have been destroyed. *Taqiyyah* relates to the branches (*furū'*) of religion; for example—performing ablution in different ways. But when the chief principles of Islam and its welfare are endangered, there can be no question of silence or *taqiyyah*. If they try to force a *faqīh*

---

[349] Abū Hurayrah: a companion of the Prophet (d. 59/679) who embraced Islam in 7 A.H. Even though his companionship with the Prophet hardly exceeded three years, he is reported to have narrated 5,374 of the Prophet's traditions, more than any other companion. Even during the Era of the Caliphate, prominent companions used to complain against him. He was named governor of Bahrain by 'Umar (but deposed later and was fined with 10 thousand dirhams due to misappropriation of public funds); judge of Medina by 'Uthmān (for whom he concocted traditions, extolling his virtues); and governor of Medina by Mu'āwiyah. It has been reported that during the Battle of Siffīn he kept aloof from taking side. Many a times he spent a day in the camp of Imām 'Ali while in the midst of Mu'āwiyah's army in another day. He used to pray behind 'Ali while giving preference to partake meals with Mu'āwiyah. He said: "Mu'āwiyah's food is more gorgeous whereas praying behind 'Ali is more virtuous." A number of traditions transmitted by him have been rejected by both Sunni and Shī'ah scholars. See 'Allāmah Sayyid 'Abdul Husayn Sharafuddīn, *Abū Hurayrah*; Muhammad Abūzahrā, *Abū Hurayrah: Shaykh al-Madīrah*; Abī Abī 'l Hadīd, *Sharh Nahj al-Balāghah*, vol. 4, pp. 63-69; Ibn Abī 'l Hadīd, *Dāyirat al-Ma'ārif Islāmiyyah*, vol. 1, pp. 418-419. [Pub.]

to mount the *minbar* and speak in a way contrary to God's command, can he obey them, telling himself "*Taqiyyah* is my religion and the religion of my forefathers"?[350] The question of *taqiyyah* does not even arise here. If a *faqīh* anticipates that by his entering the service of an oppressive government, oppression will be furthered and the reputation of Islam soiled, he must not enter its service even if he is killed as a result. There is no acceptable excuse he can offer, unless his entry into the service of the state has some rational basis, as was the case with 'Ali ibn Yaqtīn,[351] whose motives in joining state service are well-known, and with Khwāja Nāsir Tūsi[352] (may God be pleased with him), whose actions resulted in benefits also well-known.

The true *fuqahā* of Islam are, of course, free of all guilt in this respect. From the beginning of Islam down to the present, their example is clear, and shines before us like a light; they are untouched by guilt. The *ākhūnds* who joined the service of governments in past ages did not belong to our school. Not only did our *fuqahā* oppose the rulers; they also suffered imprisonment and torture because of their disobedience.[353] Let no one imagine that the *'ulamā* of Islam have ever entered the service of the state or do so now. Upon occasion, of course, they have entered it in order to bring the state under their control or transform it; were such a thing possible now, it would be our duty to do so. But that is not what I am speaking of. Our problem is the people who wear turbans on their heads, have read a few books somewhere or other (or nor read them, as the case may be), and joined the service of the government in order to fill their stomachs or increase the scope of their authority. What are we to do with them?

Those persons are not Muslim *fuqahā*; they are people whom SAVAK has issued a turban and told to pray. If SAVAK cannot force the congregational imāms to be present on the occasion of government-sponsored festivities and other ceremonies, it will have its own people on hand ready to say: "Greater be his glory!" (Yes, they have recently begun to say, "Greater be his glory" when they mention the name of the Shāh.) These persons are not *fuqahā*; the people have recognized them for what they are. A certain tradition warns us to guard our religion against these people, lest they destroy it. They must be exposed and disgraced so that they may come to lose whatever standing they enjoy among the people. If their standing in society is not destroyed, they will destroy the standing of the Imām of the Age and the standing of Islam itself.

Our youths must strip them of their turbans. The turbans of these *ākhūnds*, who cause corruption in Muslim society while claiming to be *fuqahā* and *'ulamā*, must be removed. I do not know if our young people in Iran have died; where are they? Why do they not strip these people of their turbans? I am not saying they should be killed; they do not deserve to be killed. But take off their turbans! Our people in Iran, particularly the zealous youths, have a duty not to permit these *ākhūnds*, these reciters of "Greater be his glory!" to appear in society and move among the people wearing turbans. They do not need to be beaten much; just take off their turbans, and do not

---

[350] A celebrated saying of Imām Ja'far as-Sādiq.
[351] 'Ali ibn Yaqtīn: an early Shī'ah traditionist, 124/742-182/798. His father was a staunch supporter of the Abbasids during the Umayyad period. He associated with Mansūr, the second Abbasid caliph, and is said to have assisted him in planning Baghdad. [Pub.]
[352] See n. 173 above.
[353] Although a pattern of alliance between Sunni *fuqahā* and rulers can be discerned in Islamic history, it is worth noting that there have been numerous important exceptions, e.g., Abū Hanīfah (80/669-152/769), founder of the most widespread Sunni law school, who was imprisoned by the 'Abbasid caliph Mansūr.

permit them to appear in public wearing turbans. The turban is a noble garment; not everyone is fit to wear it.

As I have said, the true *'ulamā* of Islam are free of all guilt in this respect; they have never joined the service of the government. Those who are affiliated with the government are parasites trying to grow fat on religion and on the *'ulamā*, but they have nothing to do with the *'ulamā*, and people recognize them for what they are.

We too have difficult tasks facing us. We must improve ourselves spiritually and improve our way of life. We must become more ascetic than before and completely shun the goods of this world. All of you must equip yourselves to protect the divine trust that has been vested in your. Become worthy trustees, and hold the world in less esteem. You cannot be like the Commander of the Faithful ('a), who said that the world was no more to him than the snot of a goat; but turn away from the desire for worldly gain, purify your souls, turn toward God Almighty, cultivate piety. If your purpose in studying is—God forbid—to secure your future livelihood, you will never become *fuqahā* or trustees of Islam. Prepare yourselves to be useful to Islam; act as the army for the Imām of the Age in order to be able to serve him in spreading the rule of justice. The mere existence of righteous people has a beneficial effect on society—as I myself have observed, one becomes purified by walking with them and keeping company with them. Act so that your deeds, conduct, character, and aversion to worldly ambition will have an uplifting effect on people. They will imitate your example, and you will become models for them and soldiers of God. Only thus can you make Islam and Islamic government known to the people.

I am not telling you to abandon your studies. Indeed you must study, become *fuqahā*, devote yourselves to *fiqh*, and not permit *fiqh* to decline in the centers of the religious institution. Unless you are *fuqahā*, you will not be able to serve Islam. But while you study, be concerned, too, with representing Islam accurately to the people. Islam is now a stranger; no one knows Islam properly. You must convey Islam and its ordinances to the people so that they understand what Islam is, what Islamic government is, what prophethood and imamate mean, and in the broadest terms, why Islam was revealed and what its goals are. Thus Islam will gradually become known, and, God willing, an Islamic government will one day be established.

Let us overthrow tyrannical governments by: (1) severing all relations with governmental institutions; (2) refusing to cooperate with them; (3) refraining from any action that might be construed as aiding them; and (4) creating new judicial, financial, economic, cultural, and political institutions.

It is the duty of all of us to overthrow *tāghūt*; i.e., the illegitimate political powers that now rule the entire Islamic world. The governmental apparatus of tyrannical and anti-popular regimes must be replaced by institutions serving the public good and administered according to Islamic law. In this way, an Islamic government will gradually come into existence. In the Qur'an, God Almighty has forbidden men to obey the *tāghūt*—illegitimate regimes—and encouraged them to rise up against kings, just as He commanded Moses to rebel. There are a number of traditions encouraging people to fight against oppressors and those who wish to pervert religion. The Imāms ('a), joined by their followers, the Shi'ah, have always fought against tyrannical governments and illegitimate regimes, as one can easily see by examining their biographies and way of life. Most of the time they were subject to the pressures of tyrannical and oppressive rulers, and were compelled to observe *taqiyyah* out of extreme fear---not fear for themselves, of course, but fear for their religion, as is evident from an examination of the relevant traditions. Tyrannical rulers, for their part, stood in terror of the Imāms. They were aware that if they gave the Imāms the slightest opportunity, they would rebel and deprive them of their life, which was synonymous with pleasure-seeking and licentiousness. This is the reason we see Hārūn arresting Imām Mūsā ibn Jaʿfar[354] (ʿa) and imprisoning him for several years, and after him, Maʾmūn[355] transporting Imām Ridā (ʿa) to Marv[356] and confining him there for many years before finally poisoning him. Hārūn and Maʾmūn acted as they did not because the Imāms were *sayyids*—i.e., descendants of the Prophet—and the rulers were opposed to the prophet; indeed, both Hārūn and Maʾmūn were Shīʿah.[357] They were motivated entirely by considerations of state: they knew that the descendants of ʿAli laid claim to the caliphate and that their earnest desire was to establish an Islamic government, considering this to be their duty. One day, it was suggested to Imām Mūsā ibn Jaʿfar that he delineate the boundaries of Fadak[358] so that it might be returned to him. According to a certain tradition, he drew a map of the entire Islamic realm and said, "Everything within these boundaries is our legitimate right. We should rule over it, and you are usurpers." The tyrannical rulers thus saw that if Imām Musa ibn Jaʿfar were free, he would make life impossible for them and might lay the groundwork for a rebellion and the overthrow of their rule. So they did not give him the slightest opportunity. Have no doubt that if he had had the chance, he would indeed have rebelled and overthrow the ruling usurpers.

Maʾmūn similarly kept Imām Ridā under surveillance, cunningly and hypocritically addressing him as "Cousin" and "Descendant of God's Messenger" out of fear that one day he might rise and destroy the foundation of his rule. Since he was indeed a descendant and a legatee of the Prophet (s), he could not be allowed to go free in Medina. The tyrannical rulers desired rule and were ready to sacrifice everything for its sake; they had no personal enmity with anyone. If—God forbid—the Imām (ʿa) had frequented their court, he would have been shown the utmost veneration and respect; they would even have kissed his hand. According to tradition, when Imām Ridā came into the presence of Hārūn, the ruler ordered that the Imām be carried on horseback all the way to his throne and showed him all possible veneration. But when it was time to distribute the shares that were to be given from the treasury and it was the turn of the Bani Hāshim to receive their share, Hārūn awarded them only a very small amount. His son Maʾmūn who was present was surprised as the contrast between the veneration he had just witnessed and the allotment he now saw being made. Hārūn told him: "You do not understand. The Bani Hāshim must remain in this state. They must always be poor, imprisoned, banished, afflicted, even poisoned or killed; otherwise, they will rise up against us in revolt and ruin our lives."

The Imāms (ʿa) not only fought against tyrannical rulers, oppressive governments, and corrupt courts themselves, they also summoned the Muslims to wage *jihād* against those enemies. There are more than fifty traditions in *Wasāʾil ash-Shīʿah*,[359] the *Mustadrak*,[360] and other books calling on the Muslims to shun tyrannical rulers and governments and to fill with earth the months of those who praise them, and threatening anyone who does so much as lend their panegyrists a pen or fill their inkwells. In short, the Imāms have given orders that all relations with such rulers be

---

[354] See n. 88 above.
[355] Maʾmūn: Abbasid caliph from 198/813 to 218/833, and persecutor of Imām Ridā (see n. 48 above).
[356] Marv: a city in Transoxiana.
[357] Maʾmūn and his father Hārūn were Shīʿah in the sense that they implicitly recognized the authority of Imām Ridā in their dealings with him.
[358] Fadak: see n. 134 above.
[359] *Wasāʾil ash-Shīʿah*: see n. 105.
[360] *Mustadrak*: see n. 159 above.

severed and that no one collaborate with them in any way. In contrast to these traditions are others that praise the learned scholars and the just *faqīh*, and emphasize their superiority over other men. Taken together, these two classes of traditions form a program for the establishment of an Islamic government. First, the people are induced to turn away from the tyrannical government of the oppressors and destroy their house of oppression; then the houses of *fuqahā* are to open their doors to the people: *fuqahā* who are just and ascetic and who fight in God's way to implement the laws of Islam and establish its social systems.

The Muslims will be able to live in security and tranquility and preserve their faith and morals only when they enjoy the protection of a government based on justice and law, a government whose form, administrative system, and laws have been laid down by Islam. It is our duty now to implement and put into practice the plan of a government established by Islam. I hope that by presenting the system of government and the political and social principles of Islam to broad segments of humanity, we will create a strong new current of thought and a powerful and popular movement that will result in the establishment of an Islamic government.

O God, foreshorten the arms of the oppressors that are stretched out against the lands of the Muslims and root out all traitors to Islam and the Islamic countries. Awaken the heads of the Muslims states from their deep sleep so that they may exert themselves on behalf of their people's interests and renounce divisiveness and the quest for personal gain. Grant that the younger generation studying in the religious colleges and the universities may struggle to reach the sacred aims of Islam and strive together, with ranks united, first, to deliver the Islamic countries from the clutches of imperialism and its vile agents, and then to defend them. Grant that the *fuqahā* and the scholars may strive to guide and enlighten the minds of the people, to convey the sacred aims of Islam to all Muslims, particularly the younger generation, and to struggle for the establishment of an Islamic government. From you is success, and there is neither recourse nor strength except in God, the Exalted, the Sublime.

Printed in Great Britain
by Amazon